OF THIS WORLD

Also by Joseph Stroud

Country of Light
Below Cold Mountain
Signatures
In the Sleep of Rivers

LIMITED EDITIONS

Ukiyo-e
Three Odes of Pablo Neruda
Burning the Years
Unzen

Of This World

JOSEPH STROUD

New and Selected Poems 1966–2006

Copper Canyon Press

Port Townsend, Washington

Cover art: Martin Johnson Heade, *Cattleya Orchid and Three Brazilian Hummingbirds*, detail, 1871. Oil on wood, 13¾ × 18 inches. Gift of The Morris and Gwendolyn Cafritz Foundation. Image courtesy of the Board of Trustees, National Gallery of Art, Washington, D.C.

Copper Canyon Press is in residence at Fort Worden State Park in Port Townsend, Washington, under the auspices of Centrum. Centrum is a gathering place for artists and creative thinkers from around the world, students of all ages and backgrounds, and audiences seeking extraordinary cultural enrichment.

COPPER CANYON PRESS
Post Office Box 271
Port Townsend, Washington 98368
www.coppercanyonpress.org

for
Ellen, Sam, Rachel, Charis, Mike, Tim

Some of the poems in this work were originally published in *Choice* and *Ironwood*, and in chapbook special editions from Tangram Press. "Provenance" was selected for a Pushcart Prize. "Lazarus in Varanasi," "Glad Day," and "Praxis" originally appeared in *Narrative* magazine.

I would like to acknowledge and thank the following, whose support, guidance, or critical eye have informed and influenced many of these poems over the years: Henri Coulette, John Logan, Jack Gilbert, Kenneth Rexroth, William Dickey, George Hitchcock, Stan Rice, Phil Dow, Bill Siverly, Robert Sund, Mort Marcus, Kirby Wilkins, Ellen Scott, Michael Hannon, Jerry Reddan, Sam Hamill, Dennis Morton, Len Anderson (& Rosie's-house-by-the-sea group), and especially Rachel Harris. My deep gratitude as well to Michael Wiegers, my editor, and all the good people at Copper Canyon.

Contents

3

VOICES / HOMAGES

4

DAYBOOK, NIGHTBOOK: SHAY CREEK

5

ALL THE ROOMS ARE BURNING

6

PLAINSONG

And of this world, what did you see?
What did you make of your life?

I

SUITE FOR THE COMMON

The Magician

Across the ravine from the mill house there's a grassy patch
where Gypsies keep a donkey tied to a tree. Sometimes
I'll cross the stream and bring him an apple, holding it out
like a rare jewel. He'll contemplate it, then take my whole
hand into his lips as soft as suede, and I can't tell how he
does it, but when his head lifts back, the apple has disappeared.

Night in Day

The night never wants to end, to give itself over
to light. So it traps itself in things: obsidian, crows.
Even on summer solstice, the day of light's great
triumph, where fields of sunflowers guzzle in the sun—
we break open the watermelon and spit out
black seeds, bits of night glistening on the grass.

Homage to Rolf Jacobsen

The yellow jacket keeps crashing against the pane
trying to get out. All along it's only a matter
of opening the window, finding the words,
and you're out there — in the other, larger world.
To the dead, paradise is the sidewalk you stroll down
looking in windows, humming, stopping for coffee.

Homage to the Black Walnut
in Downtown Santa Cruz

Late afternoon, trudging from the bank to the bookstore,
I stop and look up at the black walnut on Cedar Street,
into its green canopy of leaves and immense curving limbs.
A tree is a place, not an object, it's an island in the air
where our sight may live awhile, unburdened
and free from this heavy, earthen body.

Mercy, Mercy

In Lombok I woke to what felt like the knick of razor blades
on my scalp. I grabbed a flashlight—and there on the pillow
where my head had been—a half-circle of cockroaches,
the color of burnt butter, sitting in full lotus, antennae
weaving mantras, on their faces the beatific smile
of Samantabhadra, the bodhisattva of merciful kindness.

That Life Is a Circle of Heraclitean Fire

Not an original observation, but it's what I thought
when I saw lotus flowers floating on the surface of a pond
and the village girls were catching little flames of dragonflies
and stringing them around their waists and the emerald
on the lily pad changed to a frog that jumped and disappeared
into the black water out of which the jewel in the lotus blossoms

The First Law of Thermodynamics

He was a good ole boy, and when he died his friends carried out
his final wish—the body was cremated and the ashes stuffed
into shotgun shells. They walked through the woods he loved
and fired aimlessly into the trees—he came down everywhere
in a powdery rain, a pollen of ashes that once was the memory
of a boy walking under trees showering him with leaves.

Chaos Theory: Equation

The sun multiplied by bees equals honey and the addition
of leaves with rain is the sum of nights in summer
when pines ooze the resin time turns to amber
on the necklace around the throat of the woman
dividing her past by mornings in the spell of flowers
factored by the love marriage makes of yearning & desire

The Orchard

In the spring night the petals are luminous and look like stars,
each tree a pulsing, bright nebula. Summer, the limbs sag
with the weight of apples, *golden delicious* hanging like globes
of small suns, a fusion of sugar in their core. The windfall apples
are crushed and pulped into cider, the liquid a rich amber
the color of the moon rising slowly in the thick, autumn dusk.

All Through the Night the Mockingbird Sang

Of course there's no coffee, I forgot to buy some, and dammit,
Sam lost the key to the lock on his bike, I'll have to drive him
to school, I'm running late myself, the car's nearly out of gas,
I'll have to stop and fill it—auguries, omens of the day ahead
I'm thinking—when I begin to hear them, faint, rising up
inside me, those all-night songs, like dark honey, like psalms.

Every Summer the Riots

Late spring and the nasturtiums are behaving themselves, just poking
their leaves over the flower box. But I know it won't be long now—
this morning I noticed the first tentative shoot peering out
to where sunlight floods the garden, and I can see the jeweled heads
whispering in the leaves—soon they'll make a break for it, soon
the tendrils will bolt across the deck, swarming toward light.

Lost

The deer turns his head away from me and casually
continues along the ridge not even glancing back
to where I stand, to where I begin to walk across
a field of snow inside my body and lose myself
as a white ash drifts from the sky filling my tracks
and there is no way to find my way back.

Love in the Classical World

Suddenly there was Ellen's favorite hen shrieking
and rising into the air clutched in the single talon of a hawk.
Or the night the raccoon exploded out of the henhouse
with a hen in its mouth. How beautiful, how elegant,
how perfect the shape of an egg. Ellen gathers them
every morning, holds one above the skillet, breaks it open.

Biophysics

Photographs on the refrigerator held in place by magnets —
one of Sam, seven years ago, climbing out of the Grand Canyon.
The same boy who that summer caught his first cutthroat, stunned
by the iridescence of skin in sunlight. Who enters the house now
in the almost body of a man, jerks open the fridge door, and stares
hungrily — ravenous for *anything* in this world there is to eat.

Hear That Phone Ringing?
Sounds Like a Long-distance Call

Death is talking on the phone, long-distance to somebody,
I'm outside the booth, waiting to call home, impatient,
trying not to be obvious about it, while Death yammers on,
now and then looking over in my direction, his empty gaze
not meant for me, I hope, as I think of that poor guy
on the other end, clutching his phone, not ready to hang up.

What She Told Me in Orland, California

My son's a sheriff. He'll find a dead possum on the road—
if it's male he'll cut the penis off—there's a little bone in there—
then he'll boil the meat off it, and stick this sharp penis bone
in his hatband. Uses it for a toothpick. I swear to you
it's a man's world. But if I'm ever reborn—a snake, a kangaroo—
whatever—it damn well better not have a penis along with it.

The Life of a Dog

Marie understands: *Go get your rug! Want to go for a ride?*
Time to eat! Where's your toy? BAD dog! GOOD dog!
But she has problems with *Come back here! Don't jump*
on the guest! At times when we're alone, when she's looking
pensive, I'll say to her slowly and sadly, *What do you think*
of existential angst? She'll look up and her tail will wag & wag.

The Life of a Dog: Lethargy

Poor Marie, this heat sprawls her in the shade,
too hot to even nudge the jay bathing in her bowl, so
to cheer her I chant Kit Smart's poem to his cat Jeoffry,
For he can spraggle upon waggle...! but Marie just sighs,
nothing moves her—not the jay, Jeoffry, or poetry,
not even the fleas playing leapfrog on her body.

Matar la Noche

I'm in a taverna eating *tapas* and drinking a glass of wine
listening to Pepe tell me of the Spanish way: *Each moment*
is to be savored. We drink to make the mind sparkle, not
to get drunk, like those Germans yesterday—two hours
and the night was finished for them. They're very good
at making money, but we can teach them how to spend it.

The Nightingales of Andalucía

He begins to tell me about the nightingales singing in the ravine:
—Oh yeah, they're there. You see, the female's on one side
and the male's on the other, and she says, *Look, you silly bastard,*
get over here and fix this nest. If you think I'm going to lay eggs in it,
you're nuts. And he says, *Can't right now, Honey.* And she says,
Well then, fuck off. That's what the nightingales are singing.—

And I Raised My Hand in Return

Every morning for two weeks on my walk into the village
I would see the young goat on the grassy slope above the stream.
It belonged to the Gypsies who lived in the plaza below the castle.
One day on my walk back to the mill house I saw the little goat
hanging from a tree by its hind legs, and a Gypsy was pulling
the skin off with a pair of pliers which he waved to me in greeting.

Hacedor

After a lifetime of leaning over his guitar,
Segovia offered this aesthetic of craft: *Not more,*
not less. When approaching the romance of spirit,
Put on the brakes. Too much music, isn't music.
Be calm. Let the word do its work. Allow
each string its resonance in silence.

He Asked, and We Began the Train into the Heart

I settled into the compartment. It would be three days from Benares
to Madras. The Hindu across from me smiled, but we didn't speak.
Everyone, everything I knew, was on the other side of the planet.
I had no life I could call my own, no miracles, no cure. 100 miles
into the oldest, most worn-out landscape I had ever seen, the man
clapped his hands softly together—*And so, shall we speak of love?*

My Father Died

I put down the phone. I put down the phone.
What is there to hold on to? Now grief
will have its way. There is a great machine
in the blackness that dismantles one moment
from the next. It makes the sound of the heart
but is heartless.

The Others, O Lord, for My Time Has Not Yet Come

In a room of the Prado many people stop to gaze
at Brueghel's *The Triumph of Death*, a window
into the nightmare of plague—a great battlefield
where Death's legions begin the massacres.
Like everyone, I search for myself among the living,
the ones fleeing, among those trying to escape the canvas.

I Was Not Prepared for the Death of My Father

On the plains of La Mancha I met Don Quixote. I wanted
to tell him I was fleeing my father's death. In the train to Toledo,
into the light of El Greco, in the rain falling over the Tagus,
in the olive, the cathedral, I had fled. And finally into Cervantes—
I would join Sancho, I too would serve the knight, and ride
to Montiel. *Someone, please. Close the book. Leave me there.*

In the Maze Garden of the Generalife

In the Arab quarter below the Gypsy caves of Sacramonte,
Lorca heard a lament flashing like a blade — the *cante jondo*
of Andalucía where *death drifts in and out the tavern*
with the keel of the moon. Grief is a true labyrinth. I enter
the maze on the Hill of the Sun, threading the memory
of my father through each day of the years to come.

He Told Me to Come Back and See

I returned to the farmhouse where twenty years ago I watched
as Pete ground a walnut into the earth with his boot.
He smiled at me then, as if he knew some important secret.
And sure enough, in that spot there's now a large walnut tree.
Pete's been dead ten years. Back then I knew little about love,
of choices, or the great limbs that live inside the seed.

Love's More Difficult Translation

About five years into the marriage
he thought his heart had finally translated it.
But it was like that night at the Foreign Film Festival
halfway through a movie when suddenly
it switched from subtitles to dubbed English
& for an instant he thought he understood Romanian.

The Song of Divorce

Bitter the warmth of sunlight, and bitter the taste of apple,
the song and the stars and wheat fields, bitter the memory,
moonlight, the shine of the lake's surface in morning
like a sheen of pearl, bitter the hummingbird's throat
and gold pollen, all poems and their music, harp wood
and sandalwood, *bitter*, silk sheets, fire, the marriage.

In This Flesh

The bluebottle fly lit next to the scratch on my arm
and with its probing tongue began to sip at the blood—
what Hamlet would call a *reechy kiss*. I brushed it away
into its brief world stewed in corruption where the sun breeds
maggots in a dead dog. *No more marriage*, Hamlet told Ophelia.
No more honeying and making love over the nasty sty.

Where Language Fails

It's a parade coming down the street and everyone gathers
on the sidewalk to watch—troubadour poets, W.B. Yeats,
even Mandelstam's there looking a bit wild-eyed. The band's
playing *Alexander's Ragtime Band*. This is the way it is when
I'm with you. *Love* isn't the word for it. Here comes the man
with the cymbals—where they *clash* is how you live in me.

In Puerto Vallarta Once

And then we're in her room and she's unbuttoning her blouse—
we're both wrecked—sunlight shouts on the bed—dazzling—
and she begins to take off her earrings, miniature skeletons
that do a little jig as her fingers unclasp them—she wants me
to take her—*Look at me, I'm wet*—and then she crouches
and puts her mouth against the buckle of my belt—

Reading Cavafy Alone in Bed

I, too, remember the past, my room lit by candles,
and the night she entered and touched my face
with her face, with mouth and tongue and lips,
in the orchard night, in the odor of fruit,
her breasts—remember, body?—that room,
remember?—our cries, the flickering candles?

Altair and Vega Crossing the River of Heaven

Who hasn't desired a celestial love?
The *Man'yōshū* gives us Weaver Girl
and Shepherd Boy, heavenly lovers
coming together one night each year.
Hitomaro, weeping, could not sweep
all the leaves falling on his wife's grave.

Swath

Over there in the ditch, rank with vetch
and scarlet runner, tarweed, seeds blistering
in the heat, that's where it begins, that's where
we come apart in our great bed, stripping clothes
from our bodies, spilling cries under the sweep
and threshing arc of the scythe.

Iris

After Lennon died, Melissa planted bulbs.
When they come up, when they bloom,
she said, *you'll think of him.* But mostly
I remember her, Melissa, who comes back
at strange moments, a presence, like those iris
rising as blue flames out of the earth.

Cathedral

I put the shell down and wait for the snail
to emerge. I have much to learn of patience.
I no longer wonder where did love go,
or why the nights are so long. Issa says
the words will find a way across the page,
they will make a path into morning.

Idle

The *perezoso*, slow bear, what we call the sloth,
who hangs from limbs upside down and never moves
for days, its long fur dangling with moss, and when
at last it turns its slow head to peer at you, you've already
given away everything you own, you've planted yourself,
arms becoming limbs, your spirit unsheathing in leaves.

Come and Get It

So little. So much. Seasons. The orchard snowing
with blossoms. Night fall and day break. Systole.
Diastole. The path leads into the woods to the house
where the old woman invites you in to admire her oven.
Don't go! we plead—we who have been cooked
and eaten, we who sit here gripping our forks and knives.

In the Body of the Dragon

Hawthorne thought the human heart was a chamber
and if you devised the key to open it you might find
a dragon. Or an angel. Those who see the latter
walk in summer fields comforted by the blazing
chaos of sun, bees writhing in the throats of flowers,
fingers and lips stained with the blood of blackberries.

And for This Also I Am Ashamed

Dawn, and I have to catch a bus on the outskirts of Pondicherry.
So I hire a trishaw. In the darkness I don't notice at first
the man suffers from elephantiasis, his legs huge and heavy.
He pedals so slowly we're never going to make it on time and I
shout at him to hurry as we pass the glowing coals of cigarettes
that lepers balance carefully on the stumps of their hands.

Die Schwermut

In Trakl it's always evening and autumn, blue silence,
the dark shapes of shepherds, angels, a lunar voice
of the sister, and the final gold of fallen stars. It is world's
end, a synesthesia of childhood and melancholy, a vision
which could not manage the agony of the wounded soldier
who put a pistol to his head and pulled the trigger.

The Words of Chilam Balam

On the first night of the world's last days the foreigners come.
The quetzal sings no more, the jaguar flees, the deer are headless,
trees hang with the fruit of corpses, no priests can read the signs.
Gone the great wheel with its rose on whose petals are inscribed
the book of years — now these strangers with beards and pale eyes.
Prepare now for whips and fire and blood and sorrow and sorrow.

I Ask with Grief and Anger
These Days of *Ethnic Cleansing*

Shall we enter the difficult world of Paul Celan?
Can you find the key for the encryption
of his mother's execution? How do you write
out of Auschwitz? What is the journey from
shards of sapphire and lust, to his last poems,
a boot full of brain kicked out in the rain?

Lazarus in Varanasi

From a pyre on the burning ghat
a corpse slowly sits up in the flames.
As if remembering something important.
As if to look around one more time.
As if he has something at last to say.
As if there might be a way out of this.

Goya Speaks

Don't pass so quickly, my friend. What's your hurry?
Look at these paintings. See how my Colossus rises
above the world. Here's Saturn, devouring his children.
Over there, some peasants massacred against a wall.
Don't rush off. Watteau can wait. The Rubens as well.
All that frivolous beauty. Why delude yourself?

The Executions on Príncipe Pío Hill

I stand before the Goya in the Prado,
so close all I can see is paint, but if I step back,
a scene appears — men against a wall, soldiers
aiming rifles — so I keep stepping back —
across an ocean, across time, backing away,
hoping it will focus into something I can bear.

Quantum Pearls

Now it's the New Physics that tells us we don't die
at death, the body recomposes into something
rich and strange, a quantum exchange of atoms —
incandescent starlight, emerald fire in wave crest —
what Shakespeare knew all along — *of his bones*
are coral made, those are pearls that were his eyes.

Closing This Year's Anthology, I Think
of Radulfus Glaber, Who Sought Refuge

and peace from the monks at St. Germain d'Auxerre,
and they took him in, gave him soup, a straw pallet,
allowed him to stay, and for his service assigned him
a hammer and chisel to wander among the graves
of the Brethren, recarving the scarred inscriptions,
chiseling the worn names deeper into stone.

After the Opera

Coming out of the theater surrounded by people
in elegant clothes, jewelry, all the arias finished, no one
able to hold the music inside for long, soon enough
it's gone, and it's night in the city, it's all neon and noise,
the woman you're with stops to adjust her shoe, leans
her body against yours for a moment, balancing.

From Time to Time Turning My Head to See

In the washed-out arroyo through the old part of town,
below the level of the streets, & full of trash, broken bottles,
I saw one day while driving the road to Tomatlán
the huge head and bulk of a bull elephant standing
in a pool next to the burned-out wreck of a car and a woman
over and over whipping clothes against an enormous boulder.

Memory: Quonset Hut, Rodger Young Village, 1947

My mother stands next to the gas heater
in her nightdress—which suddenly catches fire,
quick bright flames rippling, unpeeling her gown,
as my father slaps at her, smothers her in his arms,
the two of them swaying there together, embracing
for the first and only time I can remember.

In My Father's Mansion There Are Many Rooms

But what about that small room
down the hall, the one with the sign—
Do not disturb—the room my mother
went into, my father, only yesterday
it seems, the room where the door locked
from within, the dead bolt sliding shut.

Babette

This is where they lived, Babette and her family, all of them
gone now, Babette with her red hair and freckles, tormented
by the boys in second grade, Babette who never made it
into history, whose life mattered only to a few, Babette,
a brief incarnation, who grew into a woman, then vanished
from my life, and from yours, O my sisters and brothers.

Missing

I keep looking for my face to appear on a milk carton,
a photo of little me, missing since '52 or '53, who left home
without saying goodbye, left his brothers playing baseball,
left his parents glancing up from breakfast, wondering at this
solitary son who sets out every morning, and returns slightly
more lost, each time less of the child he left home with.

Earth Angel

We were like children. It made little difference
who we were dancing with, just holding a girl close
for the first time and shuffling to the music was enough
in our strange new bodies, listening to the lyrics
of heartbreak and yearning—it was like paradise—
walking home with my twin, neither of us speaking.

Can You Hear It?

What is the sound the spirit makes when the body
walks across the plaza of a white village in Andalucía,
when the mind gazes out across the rooftops of Siena
among the swallows and the many shades of dusk?
The dog rises suddenly out of sleep, cocks her head,
gazes toward the door, listening to the other side.

Lost in Translation

The ten thousand leaves of the *Man'yōshū*.
Page after page of *mist*, and *dew*, and *tears*.
All those poems with their exquisite grief.
And how hard to tell from the translation
which sorrows are merely literary, which
written in an ink crushed from the heart.

Melancholy Lu Yu Returns from the Graveyard

I've been reading Lu Yu, the Master of Woe.
I know there's no end to sorrow, but good grief
he wrote 11,000 poems! My favorite is the one
returning from the graveyard when he finds his son
reading a book, laughing. Hey, I laughed, too,
and thank Buddha, so did sad old Lu Yu.

Go Fetch It!

Intelligence in animals is often measured by their capacity
to amuse themselves when alone. In this they resemble
poets. We too know how to bury the bone and then return
surprised that we have found it. We have no tail to wag,
but when the Muse says *Bark!*—we bark. We roll over.
We're as happy as the dog who gets to ride in the car.

Silence, Cunning, Exile

At Joyce's burial, the tenor sang—*addio terra,*
addio cielo. In the madhouse his daughter cried,
What's he doing under the ground, that idiot?!
When will he decide to come out? His wife
thought Joyce would be pleased with the lions
roaring each sunrise from the zoo near his grave.

Glad Day

Bees have built a hive in the wall of my shack.
I don't want to argue anymore about prosody.
I don't want to discuss Saussure, or the meaning
of meaning. All I want is to imagine those bees
making a honeycomb inside my life—all I want
is the unbelievable taste of that wild honey.

Praxis

The *Kokinshū* says poetry should move earth
and heaven, stir the feelings of the unseen gods,
soften the relations between man and woman,
and soothe the heart of the fierce warrior. Well,
of course! But poets know the really tricky part
is getting from one line to the next after they start.

Reading Wallace Stevens

I close the book and look out the window
up the hillside from the cabin where a stag
and two does pass through the sunlight
and through shadows between the pines,
disappearing among the colors they are,
appearing among the colors they are not.

If Only the Dreamer Could Change the Dream

Bly asked me if I had seen Logan recently.
No, I said, surprised, *John died... he's dead.*
Bly gave me one of his owlish looks. *In dreams,*
he asked, *has he visited you in your dreams?*
No, I said. John and I were friends in this life.
And I miss him. I miss him even in my dreams.

The Years like Crows Coming Home to Roost

Outside my window a single crow over the grove
forty years ago and when I look again there are legions
winging into the trees, their shapes like sable embers
flaming into black tongues, squalling among themselves
in the raucous unspeakable syllables of some primal,
alien world, cawing down the night to cover them.

Waking on the Shining Path

Riding the night bus to Ayacucho, jouncing,
lurching into sleep, dreamless, and then suddenly
waking, like dropping off a cliff, the bus stopped,
a village square somewhere, the driver is shouting
at a man who's waving a pistol, outside the window
ghost limbs of trees fluorescent in the streetlamp.

In Sepia

She would comb her hair sitting on the edge of the bed
in her nightgown—long, pure strokes, again and again,
pulling through snarls until the hair sheened with light—
Watching her, her calm face, arms raising, lifting her breasts,
I can remember thinking, believing—*So this is the happiness
I've come to—this is my life—this, too, is what I live for.*

This Waiting

All morning I've been watching a bee among the trumpet vines
thrumming from one bud to another, brushing against them
as if desire alone would make them bloom. All morning
I've been waiting for the poem to appear as it did for Rumi
when he beheld Shams of Tabriz, the Beloved, and words
opened like daybreak, like chords of fire within his body.

Love like a Catch of Fire

I think of Lady Izumi's poem mourning the death of Atsumichi,
how consoled she would be if only she could see his face
once more, even for a moment, as in a flash of lightning—*Seen
Unseen*. One thousand years ago, and love has not changed.
I never saw the oriole in the green leaves, just a flash of gold.
Do you think the morning won't come when you'll wake alone?

These Nights, Passing Through

Between us and death are all the days and nights
from which we fashion our life. Don't bother
to count them. They won't add up to enough.
All evening I've been listening to Netania Davrath
singing songs from the Auvergne, the music
quieting in me, the way stars dissolve in the dawn.

Dissolving

Standing above the ghats, looking down on the river,
the bodies burning, my own thoughts burning,
remembering the silk merchant in the chowk
unrolling a bolt of cobalt fire over the floor,
pouring chai into a clay cup, smiling, offering me
a nugget of sugar to place under my tongue.

No Lexicon

When I arrived, the table had already been set—plates
from China, crystal, silverware, two burning candles.
From the kitchen the aroma of basmati, cumin, ginger.
She stood in the doorway. A summer evening. A feast.
To that moment I brought everything I had, and what
I had we have no word for, though some call it *hunger.*

Ezra Under the Constellation of the Dragon

And what shall I raise against my righteousness,
what put down anger, take from the root of my heart
vanity? I have wept and I have raved in the temple
the cottonwood makes of leaves, knelt down within
the day, death's other kingdom, and still the earth
would have of me, & the night come down in points of fire.

Comice

I think of Issa often these days, his poems about the loneliness
of fleas, watermelons becoming frogs to escape from thieves.
Moon in solstice, snowfall under the earth, I dream of a pure life.
Issa said of his child, *She smooths the wrinkles from my heart.*
Yes, it's a dewdrop world. Inside the pear there's a paradise
we will never know, our only hint the sweetness of its taste.

Rock Me on the Waters

Whitman says, *All has been gentle with me.* Lucky him.
Lucky the one who has no account with lamentation.
And yet of it we string the harp for a larger music.
The sun pours down honey over the bodies of lovers
who make of their bed a small boat that rocks in the sea
of morning, rocking in waves, of light and leavings.

Our Blood Is Red Coral, We Build a Bridge Over the Abyss

I don't know if Kazantzakis ever walked the mountains of Kárpathos.
Or visited the village of Ólimbos that looks down on the Aegean.
Above the pines are the orchards of stone and light. No one lives there.
But one day while walking I heard a music—bagpipe and small bells
followed by a shepherd with his goats—up there, in midsummer,
in the furnace of the sun, in that place even the gods have abandoned.

All the Leaves On Fire Coming Down

Gone past, the cantaloupe on the table,
gone from ripe to spoiled, and only today
I was going to slice it open, scoop out chunks
with a spoon, only today I was going to sit
on the grass, barefoot, shirt undone, and eat
sweet cantaloupe in the old spoilage of the sun.

The Poem

Old and weathered, like leather
out in the rain all winter, smelling
of wood smoke, bleached silver
by the days, almost ready to go
back into earth, a husk, almost
empty, filled, almost, with light.

My Lord What a Morning
When the Stars Begin to Fall

I wake before dawn, and sense my house
around me, its skeleton of fir I framed
years ago, back in the time when I believed
I could make a shelter, back in my pride,
when I boxed out a skylight so I might
watch the stars cross over me each night.

Coat of Many Colors

Death is sewing buttons, the coat
is nearly done, soon I will put on
that robe of fire, I'll wrap myself
in the sun, then all the words will blaze,
and scatter into ash, when I become
undone, when I am no one.

Simple Gifts

The sun makes sugar in the melon, gathers sweetness
in us, builds a tower of joy in the paradise we call *body*.
Everywhere I look I see voices—the loquat's pale
gold fruit, the cottonwood's leaves, sprays of lilac.
Even the mockingbird high in the walnut tree listens
to the loud bees as if within a honeycomb of music.

And the White Goat Tethered to a Fig Tree
Above the Blue Aegean

If it happens that I am to go down into the underworld—
let no one say I went willingly, without regret or tears,
if even to see Eurydice with my own eyes among the shades
or to pitch my tent in that dark world of memory and desire
and listen to Dante sing of Beatrice. Say how I struggled
leaving this world of sunlight and strawberries and night stars

PASSING THROUGH

Sleeper, Awake

                    Look—
a web strung from the lamp, moths
entombed in silk, suspended
in air, and nestled against the shade
a spider, eyes glittering
like distant stars—

                    The Gates
are burning. The City's on fire.
The Body collapses in ash. Neither song,
nor poem, nor any honeycomb of joy,
O Sleeper, shall be your coin
of passage.

Craft

The boy playing in the plaza is now being beaten
by his father. A terrible whipping and the boy is screaming,
sobbing. The other Gypsies look on with indifference,
except for a burro who has turned, still chewing, and gazes
with its large eyes from some other world. Who knows
what the child has done. The father drags him off
still howling, but without fervor now, the worst of it
over. The silence of the noon gradually returns
as the heart calms. The mind continues its labor,
chiseling away at the Andalucían light, carving out a day
in a mountain of days, working at it, considering
whether to shape the cries and the burro. Or not.

Feral

The plaza of the Gypsies. Under the ruined castle. A spring
pouring into a stone basin where burros and horses drink.
Since before the time of Cervantes. A taverna. Fierce
sunlight at noon. The plaza empty. Absolute stillness.
Even the cicadas stunned by the heat. A plate of olives,
goat cheese, cucumber. Cobblestones. Whitewashed walls.
A day like marble. Solstice. Crushed rosemary.
Holding on with everything I have. Wheat fields
the color of fawn. Bread. Black figs. Gripping
hard, with mind and heart clenching, holding on to
what's human. This moment. This place where I make
my strict joy.

Crossing Over and Back

How *triste* the façades of the *palacios* along the Grand Canal.
And those crowds back and forth crossing the Bridge of Sighs.
Where is the other shore? This boat goes to San Michele,
the isle of the dead. No one gets off but me and two old
Russian women. They bear flowers for Stravinsky's tomb.
We walk together among the graves searching for the dead.
Good luck, I say. They smile—*Spaseba*. The one
I'm looking for is difficult to find, as he would have wished.
Most poems fail not through craft but from a failure
of character. He said that. At last I find a simple stone
embedded in the earth—the chiseled name *Ezra Pound*.
No epitaph. No famous quote. Someone has planted
a laurel nearby, but it withers in this Venetian swelter.
I say the goodbye I have carried for many years.
What is it that I still cherish? I think to myself walking back
with those two old peasant women, kindness etched
in their faces, wondering how we have been compressed
to the elementals of language, to gestures of respect
and goodwill, to the poem's chiseled music.

The Gold Country: Hotel Leger, Mokelumne Hill, Revisited

The sound of rain on the roof was too loud.
I knew someone was making love in the next room.
I recalled all those years walking with Rachel
through the orchard, the pine forest near Uruapan,
the stones and wheat and white Greek chapels of Kárpathos,
walking, it seemed, as if there were some place to get to.
I could feel the city within me begin to break apart,
all the careful bridges, the pavilions and lanes,
that fine old hotel with its marble floors
and ebony stairs, the quiet rooms with their windows
overlooking the river, the snowy egrets, a lifetime
in praise of something larger than my life,
crumbling.
    I got up and washed my face, stood looking
in the mirror looking back into the room, the rain
louder now, wondering when I would leave, how
I would go out the door into the other city,
making my way, building this time within me
a simple bare room, one window, an empty book
of white pages, and a bed for sleeping.

Directions

How weary, stale, flat, and unprofitable
Seem to me all the uses of this world

HAMLET

Take a plane to London.
From King's Cross take the direct train to York.
Rent a car and drive across the vale to Ripon,
then into the dales toward the valley of the Nidd,
a narrow road with high stone walls on each side,
and soon you'll be on the moors. There's a pub,
The Drovers, where it's warm inside, a tiny room,
you can stand at the counter and drink a pint of Old Peculier.
For a moment everything will be all right. You're back
at a beginning. Soon you'll walk into Yorkshire country,
into dells, farms, into blackberry and cloud country.
You'll walk for hours. You'll walk the freshness
back into your life. This is true. You can do this.
Even now, sitting at your desk, worrying, troubled,
you can gaze across Middlesmoor to Ramsgill,
the copses, the abbeys of slanting light, the fells,
you can look down on that figure walking toward Scar House,
cheeks flushed, curlews rising in front of him, walking,
making his way, working his life, step by step, into grace.

Signatures

I. AFTER ACOMA

> *Gentlemen! Prince Myshkin asserts that beauty will*
> *save the world! But I assert that the reason he has*
> *such playful ideas is that he is in love... Tomorrow*
> *there will be no more time.*
>
> IPPOLIT IN *The Idiot*

A dirt road through the Sangre de Cristo Mountains.
Then down into Santo Domingo. Thunderheads
and the brief, skeletal lightning.
After Acoma.
After the grief of mud huts and drunkenness,
the dirty bars in Flagstaff,
the vista where the canyon ends
and the void begins.
To this.
One moment as in marble.
Forever clear.
The wet pines, the smell of thunder,
Santo Domingo shining ahead in the sudden sun,
and my love beside me.
That this Signature should last.
That I could hold this landscape, an island,
in me. By craft

cohere the wreckage of love.
But the language fails. Always
the heart breaks into prose, fragments
of Ippolit on the sunlit balcony,
everyone laughing as he talked on into the night,
the moon rising with Myshkin's
impossible love—the cold,
continual stone of departure.

2. BELOW MOUNT T'UI K'OY, HOME OF THE GODS, TODOS SANTOS CUCHUMATÁN, GUATEMALAN HIGHLANDS

He stumbled all morning through the market,
drunk and weeping, a young Mayan whose wife
had died. Whenever he encountered people he knew,
he'd stop and wail, waving his arms, and try
to embrace them. Most pushed him away,
or ignored him. He'd stand there like a child,
forlorn, face contorted with grief, lost
in the swarm of the market, the baskets of corn
and peppers, turkeys strung upside down,
the careful pyramids of chicken eggs, women
in their straw hats and rainbow *huipiles*,
the men smoking cornsilk cigarettes,
meat hanging from the butcher stalls
(chorizo, pig heads, tripe, black livers),
boys shouting, playing soccer in the courtyard,
the Roman priest, like a thin raven, elbowing
his way through the crowds, rain clouds
swarming from far down the coast, the sun
shattered among the pines on the high ranges,
and weaving through all of it the voices
of women singing over a corpse in an earthen house,
keening a music like distant surf breaking
within the very heart of the mountain.

3. DOCUMENTARY

Bring the camera closer in. Focus
on the burning ghat. They've finished
the ceremony around the body, are now torching
the wooden pyre. See how the tongues of flame
rise from the limbs. Zero in on the head—
hold steady—capture the skull as it bursts.
Pan down the torso, the spine in ashes, the hips
crumbling. Dolly back for the scenic shot—
the Ganges flowing past. Keep the tension
sharp, you might catch the silhouette
of the rare river dolphin. Filter the lens
to bring the blue out of the mud-silt.
Now zoom down to the middle of the river,
that small boat, the boatman dumping a child
overboard. Get his flex of muscle
as he struggles with the stone tied to the corpse.
Then back to the panorama, the vista, the storm
rushing in. Lightning flashing far off
over the river palace. The silver drizzle
of rain. A quiet glow on the water.

This steaming night in Vientiane. A filthy room,
the Laotian girl gone, lice in the bedsheets,
and the Mama-san downstairs counting the money
and the hours. Outside, gunboats cruise the Mekong,
the Pathet Lao and Royalist troops stalk the streets,
forever divorced in their deadly politic.

                                 All night
I listen to Rachel's voice on the tape,
remembering those first years when we held
and held each other through the mornings, the orchard
blossoming around us, the strawberries ripe
and blazing in the field.

                                   I think of that other marriage:
Ishmael leaning over the ship's rail, holding a rope
fastened to Queequeg, who walked the slippery back
of a whale, his flensing blade carving slabs of fat,
the sea around him churning with waves
and sharks.

                            All night the tape goes on, Rachel's words
deepening with the hours, the batteries running down,
the sound going bestial, disembodied, fading
into the laughter of soldiers and whores leaving
the White Rose, mixing with the faint, otherworld song
of monks chanting in the Dragon Temple at dawn.

5. DESERT

The sun ascending above Guanajuato,

                                   a fiery stone

over the desert. And the goats out there,
their horns curving back into the skull, rooted
like the heat.

                So you have to go down
under the tombs, to the dry, cool air of catacombs
where the bones are piled higher than your head.
Along the corridor the mummies gesticulate Death,
miming all our human postures. The woman
with shriveled breasts and leather skin, holds
in the claw of her hand the nearly perfect fetus
she must have died from, its goatlike face
blank as the moon.

                  No Tiresias
among these shades to warn of homecoming,
though you've filled your cup with honey and blood.
Climbing out of the dark, into the flowers of evening,
you know the vision of that day when all the years
will brighten in you, when the sun gives up its process
for silence, black fires, the long night
of the last house.

6. JUNGLE

for Phil Dow

This jungle house on stilts overlooking
a Samoan valley, papaya trees, bushpigs
rooting among coconut husks, vines
seething with passionflowers, skinks
skittering among roots, and all of it
a feast, a continual gorging. This jungle
will eat a carcass in hours —
worms, flies, grubs, beetles, fungus
devour everything. Even bone rots.
You walk along the beaches
in the melt of sun and sluggish heat,
amid the musk smell of decay,
your flesh oozing stinging bits of salt.
And in your room at night, blood-gnats
and mosquitoes, land crabs scuttling
over the floor, bats as big as foxes
screaming outside, everything swarming
and smothering. So much like the heart,
and the continual labor of ripping out
its lush, grieving vines, breaking open
the mush-centered fruit, paring down
to adamant, the ice diamond
of that other love.

7. PARADISE

My tracks in the snow
lead down to Sho.

RIGDZIN TSANGYANG GYATSO,
SIXTH DALAI LAMA

Tsangyang Gyatso was twelve years old
when they claimed him the new Dalai Lama.
Too late, for he had fallen in love with this world.
I can see him standing in the great Potala
among the strict monks and the immense
hanging tanka of Vajrasattva.
                         Each day
he performed the service, tended the spirit.
But at night he would slip away
and steal down to the little town of Sho.
There, in a warm, yellow room, the women
undressed for his pleasure, and there he sang
his tiny poems of love.
                         And one day left Lhasa,
disappeared, to wander the ice and cliffs,
a beggar for the rest of his life. Every New Year
there's a festival in his kingdom, where monks
carve the delicate Buddha paradise from blocks
of frozen butter. At dawn, amid the chanting,
among prayer wheels and dragon masks,

                                        paradise
is tossed into the fire, and all our butter dreams
rush out in flames.

8. PARADISE FIRES

In Klungkung two boys squat on the ground
and hold between them a rooster, its neck
stretched taut, as one with a razor
carefully opens the throat, and they
let it go, flopping and flying,
its frantic song cut short
as the blood flows out in a quiet fire.
                              That other kingdom
where the black fires don't burn. Where the dead
blaze within a wooden bull, and Rangda,
the moonfaced demon with curved, tusking teeth,
gives way to the good beast Barong, guardian
of the graveyard, as the kris dancers
roll over in the dirt, knives pressed
against their chests—unharmed, blessed.
                              Far up Mount Bratan
the women come down to bathe in the lake.
Their skin shines in the late sun, the water
flows over their breasts, and all over Bali
the night makes its music, a faint gamelan
through the rice fields. The giant sea-snake
coils tighter around the sea temple of Tanah Lot,
and the slow moon burns in its own pale flame.

Everyone was in the kitchen preparing dinner
when Ellen found her cat under the cabin deck.
It had been dead two weeks. I took a shovel
and crouched between the posts into the damp
musky piles of lumber and newspapers.
I tried to pull him out by his hind legs
from beneath a tangle of boards and chicken wire.
He wouldn't budge. Clearing the pile
I discovered he'd plugged his head into the end
of a pipe. He must have died peering
through five feet of tunnel toward the dim light
at the end. *Like the chimney of hell,*
I thought, as I pried him loose. The fur
was eaten from around his skull. He looked
like a Bosch angel—the fluffy,
bloated trunk, white-tipped delicate paws,
snarled face, teeth bared, milky eyes.
I lifted him out with the shovel and carried him
to the meadow. I had prepared myself for ugliness
and the sick-sweet smell, but not
for the worms that dribbled from his mouth.
By now the sun was going down. I buried him
with the light slanting through the madrone and pines.
When I returned to the cabin, a bluegrass tune
played on the radio, four-voice harmony,
guitar, fiddle, dulcimer, the music
weaving out through the trees as pollen

drifted in the fading shafts of light.
I thought of the good earth, and the body's
slow season. I thought of the simple death.
And the hard death. All the burials
we are called to. The songs we make,
our brief harmony—*Love*,
O careless love—into your company
I work my life.

10. SOLSTICE

The gold wine of Kos. Late afternoon
below the Asklepion
                         dreaming of those Berkeley
summer evenings, those quiet, clear years
I once had. Walks along the California coast
near Albion. Dinners at the Hotel du Midi.
And the night I first entered the amber glass
of *Les Enfants du Paradis*. What did I have then
that all these years since has left me
richer, and less afraid. As now
                               on this island
in a small Greek village, I sit among olive
and fig trees, surrounded by stone white walls,
everywhere the scent of lemons, and prepare
for the honeyed ruins of deep summer, for those bees
with their deadly, droning voices.

Against Surrealism

On the road to Luang Prabang an elephant in chains stands on the flat bed of a truck shifting his weight at every bend over the river and under the trees where fox bats hang that in the market you can buy skewered on sticks grilled and dipped in a sauce of chilies and crushed limes next to river monitors living dragons their hind legs sewn together flicking blue tongues toward a stall stacked with bamboo cages the size of fists each with a swallow inside a gift for the New Year when you walk to the edge of the Mekong and make a wish opening the little cage like opening your fist your hand suddenly bursting with song

The Potato

Three days into the journey
I lost the Inca Trail
and scrambled around the Andes
in a growing panic
when on a hillside below snowline
I met a farmer who pointed the way—
Machu Picchu allá, he said.
He knew where I wanted to go.
From my pack I pulled out an orange.
It seemed to catch fire
in that high blue Andean sky.
I gave it to him.
He had been digging in a garden,
turning up clumps of earth,
some odd, misshapen nuggets,
some potatoes.
He handed me one,
a potato the size of the orange
looking as if it had been in the ground
a hundred years,
a potato I carried with me
until at last I stood gazing down
on the Urubamba Valley,
peaks rising out of the jungle into clouds,
and there among the mists
was the Temple of the Sun
and the Lost City of the Incas.

Looking back now, all these years later,
what I remember most,
what matters to me most,
was that farmer, alone on his hillside,
who gave me a potato,
a potato with its peasant face,
its lumps and lunar craters,
a potato that fit perfectly in my hand,
a potato that consoled me as I walked,
told me not to fear,
held me close to the earth,
the potato I put in a pot that night,
the potato I boiled above Machu Picchu,
the patient, gnarled potato
I ate.

Dancing with Machado

Fields of Baeza, I will dream of you
when I can no longer see you!

ॐ

Spring has come—nobody knows how.
ANTONIO MACHADO
(1875–1939)

What did I know? Baeza was just
a village in Andalucía where I decided
to stop. For I was tired of the road, of trains
and wandering. I remember the river,
the olive groves, and the distant
Sierra de Cazorla. I remember the light
above those mountains. I didn't know
what I was doing in Baeza, I didn't
know what to do with the absence
of love. Every day I walked through
the plaza and the streets, then out
into the fields. One morning I passed
a house, with a plaque on the door—

    ¡Campo de Baeza, soñaré contigo
    cuando no te vea!—
    ANTONIO MACHADO, 1915

This was Machado's house, this
was where the poet had come to live
after his wife's death, this is where

he wrote his poems of loss—*Lord,*
what I loved most you tore from me.
These were the fields he walked—
a solas con mi sombra y mi pena—
where I walked, as well, alone,
with my shadow and my grief,
where I did not have to speak.
What good was my broken Spanish,
what did I have to say? One day
on my walk through the village,
I passed a hall, and heard clapping,
guitars, a loud *staccato*, the sound
of heels stamping on a wooden floor.
Through the doorway I saw a crowd,
and a woman in the center, dancing
flamenco, one arm raised, curved,
swaying like a snake, the other
gathering the ruck of her dress—
on her face a fierce look—pride
or scorn—her heels attacking the floor
as if stamping out grief, loss, memories—
the crowd, the faces, the guitars
nothing to her, dancing somewhere
within herself, making us all
catch fire. And when it was over,
when finally I left, I took the dance
with me, took it past Machado's house,
called out to the old poet, called
for him to join me, took him along
into the fields, through the groves

toward the river. Machado danced
the color of light on the mountains—
I danced the silver of leaves—together
we danced the sun on the river—
just the two of us, two men
dancing alone in the shimmering
fields of Baeza.

The Birdcages of Oaxaca

for Bruce & Saraí Hobson

Every morning the old man set out his birdcages in a corner of the plaza. Intricate cages, beautifully crafted, carved with flowers and unearthly creatures, all of them swirling in color—lime, magenta, *amarillo*, flame—as bright as the finches and warblers within. Some of the cages were so small, so crowded, I wanted the birds released, I wanted to see them fly over the *zócalo*, and keep rising, above the tombs of Monte Albán, above the Valley of Fires. One day among the passing crowds, a young couple stopped to look at the cages. From their *traje*, their village clothes, I could tell they were Zapotec, Cloud People, from Ixtlán, perhaps just married, they seemed so young, so shy. I watched them gaze at the birds. Dear friends, there are moments when we have the chance for a simple act. I thought how I might walk over, introduce myself, offer to buy a cage and bird for them—*Con su permiso, quiero comprar por ustedes...* But how, without intruding, without seeming the rich *extranjero*, without pride or vanity? I hadn't the grace to manage it. I was young, I knew little of how to be. Nor could I imagine clearly enough those mornings, how that couple might wake and look at the cage, listen to the bird, and for a moment believe there might be, even among strangers, a kindness, a sweet charity.

Postcards to Cold Mountain

MARKETPLACE, KUALA LUMPUR

The boy with a cleaver
with one sharp stroke
chops the live crab into two
dead halves
                    spilling out oily
glistening eggs, tiny suns
Its one large claw closing
and opening

COCKPIT HOTEL, SINGAPORE

A voice "...*fuck me...yes...*" from the next room
A young Australian couple I had met at breakfast—
the way she ate her melon, shaving it
down with a spoon to where the tender, green skin
shone through

In a Land Rover
fifty miles southwest of Arnhem Land
immense marshlands, billabongs, ten thousand waterbirds
the great gene pool
genesis wonder
of wonders

Into the Dragon

Tanh and I are on Highway 1 north of Hué,
driving into the DMZ, a stretch of road
the French called *la rue sans joie*,
the wasteland we're passing was once
Quang Tri, the entire town obliterated,
wiped off the planet in 1972.
We cross the 17th Parallel, the old line
between North and South Vietnam,
the DMZ stretching all the way to Laos —
once the most ravaged place on earth,
in ten years two million tons of bombs,
and napalm, and Agent Orange.
We pass a Land Rover, a group of Brits
clearing mines and unexploded ordnance.
At a beach on the South China Sea
we come to the Vinh Moc tunnels
where a whole village lived underground,
the planes passing overhead, unaware.
Then we drive west on Highway 9
over a section of the Ho Chi Minh Trail,
to Khe Sanh, scene of the fiercest siege
of the war — General Westmoreland's *Niagara*,
where the bombs fell endlessly, one airstrike
every five minutes, for nine weeks.
Of Khe Sanh, little is left, a strip of ground
that was the landing field. A battered hangar
serves as a museum commemorating the siege.

There's a logbook with entries from Americans
who were soldiers, who have come back.
One entry reads: *Good men died here fighting
the Evil that is Communism.* 500 Americans
lost their lives in those nine weeks. Someone else
has made an entry on another page, with an arrow
pointing back: *Good men died here fighting
the Evil that is Capitalism.* 10,000 Vietnamese
died in those weeks. One of them was the father
of Tanh, who looks at the photos on the walls,
some showing the area before the war, the jungle
and rice paddies, the jagged range of mountains
running north–south, nearly the length
of the country, what the Vietnamese call
the Dragon's Back. Gradually the land
is recovering around Khe Sanh.
They're growing coffee in the hills.
On a trail in the area a sign warns —
Danger! Stay on path! UXO!
I walk the center, exactly aware
of where I place each step,
when a kid comes tumbling out of the bush,
his hands holding what look like old coins,
tarnished silver, they're dog tags, he says,
authentic, he'll sell them, along with
M16 shells, some of them live.
From his rucksack he pulls out a grenade
and offers it to me, the pin still in it.
I hold it in my hand, and stand there,
looking down on Highway 9 switchbacking

out of the hills, a logging truck gearing down,
loaded with illegal, freshly cut timber
from Laos, last of the old-growth forests
in this part of Asia. Tanh takes the grenade
from my hand. *No good*, he says,
and gives it back to the boy.
On our return, we stop at a Bru village,
hill people, impoverished, desolate, a few
wooden houses on stilts, some old women
smoking pipes, chickens scratching in the dirt,
scribbles that look like words, like numbers,
entries in a logbook, about good men,
about evil, body counts, how empty
the numbers are, how real
the bodies were, when I hear
a high-pitched screaming, as if someone
is being murdered, and under one
of the houses I see three men holding down
a pig, its front and back legs tied with rope.
One of the men swings a stone hammer
down on the pig's skull, stunning it.
He slits the throat, draining the blood
into bowls, then cuts open the body,
and the men reach inside, feeling around,
pulling out entrails. Tanh watches me
watch. I think he wants me to say
something. About the day. About
this place. Maybe about my country.
Something about people, good people,
people without blood on their hands,

if there are any, if they exist, and where
might that be, in this life, this brief
journey, this dragon world?

Speaking in Tongues

Lord Buddha, what an impossible language!
Every day I work through the phrase book—

Chào ông/bà	Hello
Có khoe không?	How are you?
Tên là gì?	What is your name?
Tên tôi là Joe	My name is Joe

But no book prepares you for the six tones
of Vietnamese—mid-level, low falling, low rising,
high broken, high rising, low broken—each
a different meaning:

ma	ghost
má	mother
mà	which
mạ	rice seedling
mả	tomb
mã	horse

So—
at the restaurant this afternoon in Da Nang
I try out my Vietnamese. I want to say—
I'd like some stir-fried vegetables and rice—
Cho tôi xin một rau xào các loại vởi cơm—
The girl taking my order can't believe
what she's just heard, she can't keep
a straight face, slaps a hand over her mouth

and rushes to the kitchen, where soon
there are loud cackles, hoots, screeches —
then a face appears from behind the curtain,
maybe the cook, an old woman looking
around for this fool who just said something
impossible, unbelievable — who knows
what I said. I settle for a bowl of *phở*
and sit looking out at the road, the sun
filtering through dust, across the way
in a rice paddy, a kid sleeping, sprawled
along the back of a water buffalo, dead
to the world. Behind him, in the distance,
Cat's Tooth Mountain, and the ruins
of My Son, the lost kingdom of Champa,
nothing but rubble now, crumbling towers,
stelae, the stone face of Shiva emerging
from jungle and shadows, lingams
pocked with bullet holes, bomb craters
filled with water, choking with lotus.
I eat my soup, and go over the rising tones,
the falling tones —

mạ	seedlings
ma	ghosts
mả	tombs
mã	horses
má	mothers

ma má mả
like the cries of a child, the elemental sound
in all tongues. I wonder what is the sound here

for *sorrow*, what syllables in this tongue for
forgive us—forgive us the terror we made—
the slaughter—horses of fire howling
out of napalm, the million tombs we left behind,
ghosts of mothers and fathers and children.
From the kitchen I still hear laughter
and the chatter in a language I will never know.
The old woman comes out once more,
a tiny, hunched crone, her teeth blackened
in the old way, comes out and watches me
eating soup. Who knows how many
of her family died in the war. Who knows
what she makes of me. She stands there
with her black smile. Then gives me a sound,
a word, in English, maybe the only one
she knows, one simple sound as I raise
the bowl to my mouth—

    Good

                      she says.
I place the bowl on the table
and look at her. I nod, and answer—

    Yes   *Good*

And then in her tongue—

    Vâng   *Tốt*

Passing Through

Hoi An — the Thanh Binh Hotel,
a cheap, grotty room. Fever,
night sweats, tongue swollen,
eels squirming in my belly,
no strength to get out of bed.
What is wrong with me?
Is this *it?* Is *this* the final passage?
For two days I look up at the fan,
three blades slicing the air.
I watch the two geckos
upside down on the ceiling.
Their golden eyes never close.
On the third day they tell me their names,
Li Po and Tu Fu.
They write poems across the walls.
The blades swish over them
and in the *thish thish thish*
I can almost hear Li Po
reciting the *Tao Te Ching.*
There's a sign on the wall next to my bed —
motorbikes firearms explosives stinking things
even prostitutes not allowed in room.
On the fourth morning I rise,
stand under the shower and let the water
stream over me.
On the fifth day I walk
down Le Loi to the Cam Nam Bridge,

past the old Chinese Assembly Halls,
their roofs carved with dragons.
Near an empty courtyard
a boy stands under a flame tree
holding a string whose other end
is tied around the thorax of an insect,
a blue-green metallic-sheened beetle
the size of a hummingbird
buzzing in slow circles around the boy's head.
From the bridge I watch fishermen
cast their nets over the Thu Bon River,
draw them in, and spill onto the beach
a thousand glittering coins.
I look to the other shore
where coming toward me
riding over the bridge on bicycles
a procession of schoolgirls
all dressed in white silk *ao dai*s
holding white parasols over their heads
floating over the slow-moving waters
like a vision of the white orchids of paradise
in the dream of a dying man.

At the Well of Heavenly Clarity

I was lost in Hanoi's Old Quarter, wandering among its maze of lanes and alleys, the Street of Knives, the Street of Graves, the Street of Silk. An old man noticed my confusion, a stooped old man, wispy beard, beret, who tapped his cane over to me. He spoke a little French, I had my phrase book, and we tried to work out where I was, where I might be going. I opened the map, pointed to the Lake of the Returned Sword, then to the Temple of Literature. Between them—a labyrinth of lines and incomprehensible words. The old man put his finger to a place on the map, then pointed down to the street where we stood. Gradually he traced a route, faced me in the right direction, and soon I was entering the gate of Van Mieu, the Temple of Literature, a thousand years ago the center of learning in Vietnam. The grounds are arranged to suggest Confucian thought. Five Courtyards reflect the elements of human nature, the path through them the Middle Way, the Golden Mean. The grounds were peaceful, quiet, a place of serenity at the center of a seething city. I had been reading about Confucius, Khong Tu, his emphasis on order, selflessness, nonviolence. For weeks I had been wandering through the past, through old wounds, battlefields, graveyards. I thought of the war tales I had heard, the story of the farmer, a suspected VC, who was taken up in a helicopter, held a thousand feet above the earth to terrify a confession from him, then let go over his village. The story of Hué, and its mass graves of civilians the VC left behind. The blood on my hands. On everyone's. I walked the grounds, and came at last to Thien Quang Tinh, the Well of Heavenly Clarity. I looked down a long time, the sky reflected in the water. A long silky contrail passed through the clouds and lily pads, a 747, streaking toward Beijing.

Not long ago the contrails were B-52s, sketching murderous, terrifying sentences across the heavens. I looked into the well, thinking of the old man on the Street of No Name. I thought of the map of the heart, the maze, the words we need to translate, from every tongue. Not the political words, but the human, the words for comrade and friend, sister, brother. I looked into the well, a few bubbles bubbling up, and then, rising from the depths, breaking the surface, a turtle, an ancient turtle, moss-backed, eyes a clouded jade, so old, so venerable looking it could have been the embodied spirit of Khong Tu, living here for a thousand years. It stretched out its neck, turned its slow, ponderous head, its beaklike mouth appearing to smile, a smile of heavenly disinterest. It turned its head a moment, looking around at the world, then sank back into the well.

Country of Clouds

Her name is Yeem,
she's a fifteen-year-old Black Hmong,
and we're in a Russian jeep climbing a road
in the mountains outside of Sa Pa.

Yeem is singing the lyrics to Bob Marley's
No Woman No Cry.
She can sing it in Vietnamese.
She can sing it in French.

We are on our way to Bang Khoang,
a remote Red Dao village
near the border
where China crossed over in '79,

200,000 soldiers
would teach Vietnam a lesson,
and two weeks later
180,000 crossed back.

The mountains are in clouds,
a fine mist—*The breath of the dragon,*
Yeem says, and I ask her
Have you ever seen one?

She laughs, but when she was a child
she saw a cloud leopard below Fan Si Pan.

We reach a washout in the road
and the driver slows the jeep.

Yeem says something to him in Hmong
and he grunts,
shifts into compound low,
and we begin a steep climb,

the road no longer a road,
just ruts and a hacked tunnel through the jungle.
In an hour we come to a clearing
blocked off by poles of bamboo,

looks like a toll gate, there's a small hut—
a group of soldiers stand around
armed with AK-47s
and not pleased to see us.

Yeem gets out of the jeep
and begins talking to an officer,
a small man in a tan uniform.
She gestures back at me

and the officer shakes his head,
an emphatic *No.*
He walks over and looks at me,
says something to Yeem in Vietnamese.

He wants to see your passport, she says.
I don't have it with me.

Tell him it's back at Cat Cat.
She speaks to him.

The soldiers stand around,
curious, watching, no smiles.
Yeem gets into the jeep.
We go back, she says.

The driver smiles.
On the way down
she tries to tell me.
There's trouble with the hill tribes,

the Hmong, the Dao, the Zay.
In the Central Highlands there's been fighting,
maybe the beginnings of revolution,
tribal people and government forces.

She doesn't go into details.
Masking her face,
she looks away.
I don't ask questions.

We come out under the clouds
and drive the main road
toward Lai Chau Pass,
the terraced fields far below

glimmering with water
which make me think

of the ponds in the Red River Valley
on the train up from Hanoi.

Why so many, I mused then,
and it was Yeem who told me
they were bomb craters,
reminders of the American War.

We stop at the Pass
and walk up a slope
through a heavy mist
to a mound of earth on top.

At first I think it's a grave
like others I've seen in villages
but it's not.
It's a gun placement,

the ruins of a turret
overlooking Dien Bien Phu,
where the French parachuted in
and then had no way out.

Ho Chi Minh came through here
after thirty years of exile,
carrying his typewriter,
beginning the Liberation.

Yeem wants me to see
something else,

so we climb higher
until at last we come out

into a country of light
above the clouds,
the peaks of the Annamites
rising out of the mists

all down the length of Vietnam,
peak after peak
jutting out of the clouds.
From up here you can see

above everything, Yeem says.
I come here sometimes.
It's like having a clear mind.
We linger, then descend

back into the mists, into the world
where all we can see is each other
and the trail disappearing ahead
in the breath of the dragon.

Home. Autumn. The Signatures.

for Tim

I

Rain
and the first cold night
after a summer of sleeping between sheets.
Restless, I lie awake for hours
brooding on the wreckage of years.
As the storm thunders in from the Pacific,
I get up and fumble for blankets in the dark.
They smell of cedar
after months of being cramped in a dresser.
I pile them on the bed
and lie back dreaming of those nights
from my childhood
when I imagined the rumpled blankets
to be a sea churned by storms
where I sailed in my little boat
with the ocean of stars turning
outside my window.
I think of Issa's bed,
the broken-roofed shed he died in,
a drift of snow falling through the night,
and the poem they found
next to his body—

There are thanks to be given.
This snow on my blanket—
it too is from the Pure Land.

2

A doe came this morning to feed
on the last leaves of the peach tree.
She turned her face to me
and stopped. We stood there
gazing across the distance—
two creatures measuring the immense
difference of blood and star drift.
Her sloe, almost sad eyes,
the large, delicate ears
with their thin branching of veins.
In a moment, she was gone.
And when I looked again
she had stopped on the ridge,
her head turned, peering
back, before she flicked
and disappeared. *Yes,*
there must be a love
worth waiting all our life
for.

3

The garden's last ripe tomato.
I lay it on the cutting board
and with a fine-edged knife
slice it clean through.
Both halves keel over—
and there is autumn's city,
with its bloody seed-shine of canals,
bridges, tiny boats, a labyrinth
surrounding at the center the great palace
of emptiness.

4

Let the day begin with its light.
For once, let the mothers and fathers sleep late.
Let the chickens in the mud
scratch their own inscrutable chicken poetry.
Let the clothes hang from the line
in the rain.
Allow the crickets under the woodpile
one more day of their small music.
Soon everything will be clean
and bare, a fine inner blazing as the leaves
drop, and the air is tinged with oak
burning across the fields.
Let the skeletons of cornstalks
scrape in the wind
and sunflowers droop heavy heads
spilling their crowns of seeds.
Let the dew on the webs
gleam a thousand pearls
as the sun hazes its light
around everything we must lose.
Let the night build its darkness,
and the earth close once more
and, at last, become quiet.

5

Hunter moon. Clarity.
A room fashioned inside me.
Bare and clean. White walls
and one window. The short days
and the greater night to prepare for.
A leanness. The simple joy
of being still. Solitude.
The single tree with its fruit
gone. What my heart
remembers. Compassion.
What *did* Myshkin feel
lying in that room with Rogozhin
next to the body of the only woman
he ever loved?

6

I take heart in the simple act
of planting these Iceland poppies.
It's a mystery to me
how they will find something in this freezing earth
to grow out of, and flower.
It's the light of autumn I love,
an opal sheen as it pools the ocean,
the old brass of the hills,
a gathering of all the years,
and the leaves beginning their final
gold burning, letting go, going
under. The freshness the rain leaves,
the windows everywhere clear
without the reflection of things
in them. If I had my life to live again,
how could I choose more than this?
Down on my knees, hands in the earth,
I recall the valley outside Jalalabad
with its melon fields and orange groves,
where I stopped a farmer in his wagon,
bought a melon, broke it open on a stone,
and sat by the road eating the crisp,
sun-glazed fruit under the snow peaks
of the Hindu Kush. From that distant moment
to this. All the Signatures, all
the turnings through grief
and joy, the grace of this world
that allows us passage.

3

VOICES / HOMAGES

Homage to Life

"Hommage à la vie"

JULES SUPERVIELLE

It is good to have chosen
a living home
and harbored time
in a constant heart,
to have seen one's hands
touch the world
as an apple
in a small garden,
to have loved the earth,
the moon and the sun,
like old friends
beyond any others,
and to have entrusted
the world to memory
like a luminous horseman
to his black steed,
to have given shape
to these words: wife, children,
and to have served as a shore
for roving continents,
to have come upon the soul
with little oarstrokes

for it is frightened
by a sudden approach.
It is good to have known
the shade under the leaves
and to have felt age
steal over the naked body
accompanying the grief
of dark blood in our veins
and glazing its silence
with the star, Patience,
to have all these words
stirring in the head,
to choose the least beautiful
and make a little feast for them,
to have felt life
rushed and ill-loved,
to have held it
in this poetry.

Ode to the Smell of Firewood

"Oda al olor de la leña"

PABLO NERUDA

Late, when the stars
open in the cold,
I opened the door.
                    The sea
was galloping
in the night.

Like a hand
from the dark house
arose the intense
perfume
of firewood.
A visible scent
as if the tree
were alive.
As if it still pulsed.
Visible
like a robe.
Visible
like a broken branch.

Overwhelmed
by balsamic

darkness,
I went
inside
the house.
Outside
the points
of heaven were glimmering
like magnetic stones,
and the smell of firewood
touched
my heart
like fingers,
like jasmine,
like memories.

It was not the sharp smell
of pines,
it was not
the cracked skin
of eucalyptus,
nor was it
the green perfume
of vineyards,
but something more secret,
because that fragrance
exists once
only,
once only—
And there, of all that lived in the world,
in my own

house, by night, near the winter sea,
there it was waiting for me—
the smell
of the deepest rose,
the heart cut from the earth—
and something
entered me like a wave
unloosed
from time
and I was lost in my self
when I opened the door
to the night.

Autumn

from the Man'yōshū

So
it comes to this—
And we thought our love
would last a thousand years

ŌTOMO NO YAKAMOCHI

ॐ

Last night you sent me away
into the darkness—
Tonight do not make me
walk that road again

ŌTOMO NO YAKAMOCHI

ॐ

Dawn in the imperial city—
I hear the *swish* of oars
and remember those fishing girls
from long ago

ANONYMOUS

Burning the Leaves

after the Japanese & R.H. Blyth

Fifty years
watching the leaves
fall

જ

How many days
did I just let
go by

જ

Burning the leaves
under
the falling leaves

જ

Among the cliffs
a lark's song
breaks against rock

જ

The moon rises
over the grave
of my child

॰

I gaze and gaze
into an empty
bird's nest

॰

What *is* it
on the riverbank
the crow is eating?

॰

How many leaves
will fall
over my grave?

॰

Moonlight on granite
that's all
it is

॰

So busy
with busyness
I didn't *see* what I saw

～

Among the cherry blossoms
thinking
I'm among the cherry blossoms!

～

All day drinking wine
writing not one
good line

～

So hot
even the melons
squat in the shade

～

The cockroaches
running off
think I'm after them!

～

Eyes swaying on stalks
the snail looks up
into my face

༈

Moon on the river
a fisherman
casts his net

༈

Both worlds
the singing of the lark
and the silence after

Of Sappho / [fragments] / *Sabi*

neither the sweetness of honey
nor the sting of bees

_____

                                black sleep of night

_____

like a fierce wind in the oak
love shakes my heart

_____

                                evening star, most beautiful of all stars

_____

dawn woke me

_____

                                in the bright flame of noon
                                a cricket sings

_____

when we meet
death lurks close by

———————

                    take off your nightdress

———————

between us the sea glistens
and shatters with waves

———————

the hours   empty   endless

———————

                 please   that moment
once again

———————

                 gold greater than gold

———————

the moon goes down
the Pleiades

———————

                 alone
                 in a deepening night

Steps to the River

versions from the ancient
Sanskrit & Tamil

Friend
this night makes music of me
of my body
just as the wind makes flute songs
through the shining holes of bamboo
bored by those black bees
from the land where he dwells

ॐ

Her young body is like an island
Her beauty the waves that continually break upon it
There is a hidden place
a hut of tendrils and vines
in whose moist shade even now
the drowsy god of love
begins to stir

ॐ

Everyone in the village asleep
except us
all night hearing
the blue-sapphire flowers

tearing loose from branches
falling all night
as the two of us
listen

༄

Impossible to measure
my love for that man from the mountains
where the black stalk of the *kuriñci*
flowers every twelve years
and of its pollen bees make their richest honey

༄

The jingling from her anklets stops
Her lover, tired, rolls onto his back
And now the room chimes
with the sound of tiny bells
from the belt around her waist

༄

Over here the sheets smell of musk
over there a stain of henna
disheveled here, kohl marks there
crushed flowers in the blankets
everywhere clues of her postures
from the night before

༄

Lover of pollen, you are trapped
The struggling bee makes the petals
close around him

༄

They didn't speak
No art was involved
Just the touch of his hand
the loosening of her skirt
In a moment
it was over

༄

She lifted her arms to undo her hair
and glanced at me with shining eyes
I swear, friend, even the blossoms of water lilies
catch fire

༄

Dear, don't feel so smug
because he's painted your portrait
He might have done mine as well
but the brush kept trembling in his hand

༄

The one from his height looks down
believing he is great
The other from the ground looks up
believing he is poor

လ

Little cuckoo
don't sing until you can fly
The crows around here are vicious
toward any song
other than their own

လ

You gave me feet the long road wears down
You gave me a wife who left me
You gave me this body time burns to ashes
You gave me a voice for begging
Lord, when will you weary of all your gifts?

လ

Like glittering waves on water
the boasters and loudmouths
get everyone's attention
If you seek the pearl
hold your breath
and dive deep

❧

A village wall in winter
where the children of the poor
freezing in tattered rags
shove and huddle together
in the one spot the sun warms

❧

The frog clears its throat
squinches forward
and leaps
mouth open wide
toward a swarm of flies
hovering above the dungpile

❧

No money
No wisdom
No merit
The story of my life
and now the jig is up

❧

Like a heavy temple bell
struck hard
death claims a good man
And his love resonates after
shimmering through our lives

Festival

We are at the gate above the river.
Peach trees surround the pavilion.
It is the time of the Emperor's feast,
the bounty of his riches and exquisite ladies.
Over there is Li Po, drunk and sick
on rice wine. They unscroll the silk
before him. The crowd is quiet. Error
is not allowed. Li Po has to be held,
the brush shakes in his hand. Suddenly
the poem lurches out. A sword in sunlight.
Our broken machine of language at last
at flow with the river. Fireworks
and sparklers cast lights on the water.
Lamps are lit on the fragile trees.
Do you see the Emperor, abandoned and alone,
in the crowd of weeping faces?

Listening to Issa

This world of dew
and still
we fall in love

The crow walks
as if *he*
were tilling the field

I know I'm old—
but the flowering cherry trees
don't dislike me

Come on frog—
let's see you dance
to your own music

The oriole
wipes muddy feet
on the plum blossoms

Where are you
going in this *rain*
little snail?

Pissing—
I look down and see
a wild iris

The child
pulling a turnip with all his strength
topples backward

A crane
alights
on the garbage dump

In my hut
fireflies and mice
are friends

The old man
hobbles out
to look at flowers

So, moth—
this life—
are you happy with it?

How strange
to be alive
under the cherry blossoms

Am *I* next?
Is it *this* body you're cawing about
O crow?

This long night—
so very long—
praise Buddha

In every pearl
of dew
I see my home

Praise Poems

for John Logan

after Margot Astrov's
The Winged Serpent

TO THE DAY

For it begins our journey—
It is the mountain
Over our homes

TO FIRE

For it is the voice of God—
It is the bright color
Of all our children

TO WATER

For it is the way of the spirit—
It fills the footprints
Where the body has vanished

TO THE HORSE

For it leads us from this life—
It runs in darkness—
It bears us across the waters

TO THE BEAR

For it is figured in the stars—
It follows the bee's
Trail of pollen

TO THE FATHER

For he leads the way—
He is the hand of shelter—
He bears our grief

TO THE MOTHER

For she gives us to the world—
She is the happiness
We find in ourselves

TO SALT

For it comes from weeping—
It is the Saint's pearl—
Our touch of stars

TO MORNING

For it is the open door—
It is the welcome
Of all our friends

TO THE STARS

For they are seeds of light—
They are the small, pure songs
That rain upon us

Alam al-Mithral

I confess I was among the Elders
peering between the leaves at Susanna's nakedness
watching the light shine on her hair
as she washed it clean. I was there,
standing in the dust, under the cruel sun of Jeremiah.
I had come to steal the ripe figs
from Joakim's garden, for I was hungry
and my family poor. In my mind
I could taste the fruit of her. This is not
about lust. Of the Elders, I have nothing to say.
I left them at the crack in the wall
down on their knees. I have been to Aqaba
and Aleppo. I've seen the mark of Cain
on the brows of men, have heard the prophets
warn of the wrath of the Lord. I will wait
and see. Job says our days are swifter
than a weaver's shuttle and come to their end
without hope. For me, the miracle is of this body,
and in me until I lay it down I will carry
my sweet cargo, that sliver of paradise
glimpsed, once only, when I was a boy of fourteen.

Listening to Leon

My time's coming, and that's a hard thing to say, I go to bed at night
      not certain I'll be here in the morning, I got this fear lying in
      the dark, I can't sleep, and I'm scared of thinking

Every afternoon loud music from the neighbor's place, she calls it
      rap, rhymes with *crap*, but everyone's got their own music,
      it's been years since I heard *Body and Soul*, never thought
      I'd hear anything better, and I haven't, Coleman Hawkins,
      1939, Memphis, a juke joint, drinking whiskey, twenty-five
      years old, my whole body filled with music, a couple of years
      before the War

I don't know, I don't know, that's what I say, not I don't care or I
      don't think so, it's not a negative thing, no, it's not some
      loose change you get from every mother's son, I don't know,
      you know what I mean?

I miss the woman, the mornings mostly, the sweetness like a ripe
      peach, all those years reaching my hand into the leaves,
      feeling around in there for the touch, and I never knew
      when the last one was the last one

Thirty-two years I drove a bus, watched coins drop, people paying
      to get from here to there, thirty-two years to get here,
      retired they call it, but I'm not tired, I'm just old, like
      everybody else I buy my onions and carrots at the market, I
      don't own property, when I was a boy I planted some seeds,

squash and bush beans, sweet corn, in the Georgia summer,
a simple thing, a garden, some dirt and water, some sun,
some time

Walking home after the dance, you know what I mean, a bit weary
but feeling good, still hearing the music, remembering how
we danced, walking out of town, into the country, a big
night sky with stars, the music faint, but holding on to it,
remembering, humming, sometimes that's the way it is
for me

My Marriage with Death

Death joins me for breakfast at the hotel café.
He orders *huevos rancheros*, lights a cigarette,
gazes at me a moment, then opens the newspaper.
So. One of those no-conversation mornings.
We're in the sixth year of our marriage,
vacationing here in the Yucatán, an ancient culture
he knows well. I've been reading the guidebook
about the pyramids, the steep stairs to the altar,
a priest holding up to the sun a fresh pulsing heart.
I watch Death smoke and read the paper, purse his lips,
flicking ashes over his plate smeared with yolk.
I try remembering those first months of courtship,
the walks along Point Lobos, restaurants and concerts,
afternoons in Napa driving through the wine country.
My friends had warned me. Beware this older man.
This man with money and manners, with patience
and culture, a hint of cruelty like a fine cologne.
I wanted it. He made clear for me my presence
in time, how my life surrounds the moment. Even
this moment, this glass of ice water on the table,
dazzling, beaded with diamonds of light. We have
no plans for today. I'll read by the pool. Death
will be off somewhere, as usual. I no longer ask him
about it. Tonight perhaps we'll make love. I'll sit
in bed and comb my hair, the one thing that still
interests him, the only thing left that makes him sad.

What He Told Me in Phôngsali

Passport? Man, forget about your passport, you're not going to need
a passport up there, the only way in is by jeep, then upriver by boat,
from there you have to walk two maybe three days, it's in the Triangle,
you know, bandit country, guerrillas, opium fields, no-man's-land,
no borders, you can't tell if you're in Laos, Burma, China, Thailand,
Vietnam, nobody knows and nobody cares, all kinds of hill tribes,
Black Hmong, Flower Hmong, Mien, Akha, Lahu, hell, languages
nobody understands, animists, weird voodoo stuff, they eat dogs up
there, strip the skin from live snakes, milk the blood into a bowl and
drink it, some'll even drink the venom, no lie, up there even the kids
are on the pipe, look like skeletons, men hunt bushpigs with AK-47s,
you better not walk anywhere off the trails, the Americans dropped
tons of ordnance up in there, B-52s that couldn't unload over Nam
just dumped it all up there, a lot of it didn't go off, people get blown
up all the time, you'll see farmers walking around without a leg or
missing an arm, it's the dead end of the world up in there, spooky,
they say there's still cloud leopards in the mountains, last year they
found a new kind of deer, about the size of a dog, barks like one too,
got black gibbons, fox bats, gorals, pit vipers, king cobra, got leeches
the size of a buffalo's tongue, got dengue fever, liver flukes, lung-
worms, got hepatitis A, B, C, D, *and* E, malaria, typhoid, cholera,
rabies, got Japanese B encephalitis, mosquitoes carry it, a virus, eats
away the brain, they say the first symptom is visions, transcendence,
like you're waking inside the Diamond Sutra, they got *everything* up
there, so I'm telling you you won't need your passport, and don't tell
them you're American, say you're Canadian, oh yeah, be sure to tell
them you're a poet, they love poets, can't get enough poets up there,

they have poets for lunch, and if you get in a bad fix, which guaran-
teed you will, you can tell them you know me, but if I were you—no
way would I go up there—okay?

To Christopher Smart

I will praise Christopher Smart
For his life was a flame unto the Beloved
For he wrote with a key on the madhouse wall
For he slept in class and taught in the tavern
For his secret name was Mother Midnight
For in his orisons he loved the sun and the sun loved him
For he considered his cat Jeoffry
For he knelt in the street and asked strangers to join him
For he sang out of poverty and debt
For he saw the Lord daily and drank with him often
For in his nature he quested for beauty
     And God, God sent him to sea for pearls

Homage to George Mackay Brown

Who had the key to the star and the key to the grave
Who unlocked the runes in the Stones of Brodgar
Who heard the skalds of sun wreck and sea wrack
Who passed through the silver doors of the rain
Carried shipwreck and lark, snowflake and fire
Who cut the thread from the wheel of Morag
And wove Scapa Flow, the Kist, Eynhallow
Wove stars and named them

> *I am the Bringer of Dew*
> *I am the Grain of Dust from the Floor of Heaven*
> *I am the Keeper to the Door of Corn*

Who watched a ship of light crossing between islands
The rowing heavy, like lifting oars from honey
Who anchored in the taverns of Hamnavoe
Who walked in the kirkyard among names carved on stones
Who looked into a fresh-cut furrow
And saw a charred ship, oars dragging through ash and skulls
Who cast his net and brought up the little silver brothers
Brought up the cold running of stars
Who—but George Mackay Brown—
A child of time, maker and voyager
Who yoked his words to the ox of Tammag
And plowed the earth into song

Praise

Chou Pi-ta
praised the poems of Yang Wan-li,
said they seemed to be composed
in the time it takes
to walk seven steps
and yet not a word in them
can be changed,
said his poems have the power
to drain the Three Gorges,
pierce the Center of Heaven,
and penetrate the Caves of the Moon.
When told of this,
Yang replied—
Ah, Master Chou
and his shameless
modesty!

Cézanne and the Noumenal World

Dusk, gold and blues—the haystacks of Monet—his water lilies
shimmering in the texture of light. Like Debussy. Who wouldn't
eat from that plate. Or Gauguin—his islands and women
and the red flowers and blue horses and the green sea.
Van Gogh's night astonished with stars, the black of blackbirds
in yellow wheat, a sky in torches of black flame.
Seurat dabbing the tip of a brush ten thousand times
to give us the molecular blaze of figures on la Grande Jatte.
Renoir's nudes—flesh an opal fire glazed with pearl.

But it's Cézanne

who troubles me—his architecture of color, sculpture of light—
Cézanne who tried to carve the flow of the world in canvas.
His still lifes—so careful, so slow—the grapes and pears turned
before he could finish. So he turned to the mountain, every day
for years confronting Sainte-Victoire, attempting the substance
of granite, a structure outside seasons.

In his studio at the end,

an old man, dying, he hobbled over canvases strewn on the floor,
Sainte-Victoire wavering now—trees and cliffs washing out,
the great mountain inside him fading—spoiling like the fruit
on the table—alchemized in the core of the flesh.

Geode

When Zárraga visited Bonnard's room
he found the painter surrounded by light,
the sun flashing off white canvases.
Over the months they would fill with nudes
and still lifes: the light of Le Cannet accented,
exaggerated with magenta, crimson, vermilion,
as he colored his paradise.
                                    For years
I tried to see women and landscapes
through his eyes—sought to glimpse auburn
among the shade of cedars, hints of lilac
in the ferns, cobalt, the sheen of tourmaline
on her. Then I fell in love.
                                    Now I look
through a huge country of silence, tracing
the different, foreign colors of night,
working on my own canvas of a Greek island
and stone house, the valley far below
with its stark church and fields,
Rachel out on the terrace, kneeling
over the cold water, washing her hair
in the granite light.

Proportions: Homage to Brueghel

For years I've lived with Brueghel's painting
The Harvesters' Meal. At first I noticed
just the obvious—men and women sitting
on wheat sheaves, eating their simple meal
of cheese and gruel. The pensive, sad-eyed man
slicing bread, a woman lifting a pitcher of water
to her mouth.
             Then I moved on to the wheat fields,
the straw colors. The man with his curved scythe
slashing the long stalks. Another man lugging
heavy water jugs in each hand. Three women
carrying sheaves on their shoulders walk on a path
that will lead past the thatch-roofed houses
toward a grove of trees where the tower of a church
juts into the sky.
             For a long time I watched the dog
in the foreground. A spaniel of sorts,
sniffing the earth, its white tail rigid.
                         Gradually
I became attracted to the expressions on faces,
the exhaustion of work on a summer day,
I kept wanting to see the face of the young woman
with her back to me. Midway in the painting
two people pause to talk. A man and woman, I think.
Behind them two locust trees suffused with light
mingle their branches and leaves.

                                    This held my attention
for a year. Then I began to consider color,
how it blended from the greens of the forest
into the gold and amber of the fields, the blue sky
mottled with dust. I began to dwell on proportion,
harmony and balance, our burden of earth,
excess and pleasure—the long, difficult craft
of living.
            Recently I've been following
the road in the background, the way
it rounds a small hill and disappears
into what I imagine is a valley. Always
that other landscape the heart dreams
and yearns for. A place deep inside
the painting, a living realm, borderless,
a dwelling art makes within us.

Homage: Doo-wop

There's so little sweetness in the music I hear now,
no croons, no doo-wop or slow ones where you could
hug up with someone and hold her against your body,
feel her heart against yours, touch her cheek
with your cheek—and it was okay, it was allowed,
even the mothers standing around at the birthday party,
the rug rolled back in the living room, didn't mind
if you held their daughters as you swayed to the music,
eyes squeezed shut, holding each other, and holding on
to the song, until you almost stopped moving,
just shuffled there, embracing, as the Moonglows
and Penguins crooned, and the mothers looked on
not with disapproval or scorn, looked on with their eyes
dreaming, as if looking from a thousand miles away, as if
from over the mountain and across the sea, a look
on their faces I didn't understand, not knowing then
those other songs I would someday enter, not knowing
how I would shimmer and writhe, jig like a puppet
doing the *shimmy-shimmy-kokobop*, or glide from turn
to counterturn within the waltz, not knowing
how I would hold the other through the night
and across the years, holding on for love and dear life,
for solace and kindness, learning the dance as we go,
learning from those first, awkward, shuffling steps,
that sweetness and doo-wop back at the beginning.

Homage to the *Word-hoard*

Lord help me but my mind's a blank today, only a few words bubbling up, words like "no," or "glum," or "dull," but there must be thousands of others down there, rattling their cages, clamoring to get out, all kinds of words, big ones, scrawny ones, heroic and muscular ones, coy, loony words, words tasting of cloves and licorice, cross-dressed words wearing feathery boas, quantum words, kaons and koans, singularities, black hole words sucking up light, love, and loss, exploding words, supernovas, words like wormholes into other worlds, ancient words, Neanderthal words rubbing together to make fire, Cro-Magnon words rubbing together to make magic, spells, incantations to sail the dead off to the underworld, words that make the blind see, that make the lame walk, words queuing in iambs, *verse libre* words playing tennis without a net, and yes, I must admit it, bad words, embarrassing words, words I dare not mention, and ugly words, too, words with blackheads, wens, squatty warts sprouting tufts of stiff hairs, blubbery words, Jean Paul Sartre words dripping *ennui*, words smoking a cigarette, raising a Marlene Dietrich eyebrow and looking down from a great height, words you wouldn't be caught dead wearing, virgin words, cocky words, sluttish words, whispered-in-the-ear words, Etruscan words, words from lost tongues, words with fur and teeth, wolf words wandering the plain bringing down antelope, words that singe, sing, and burn, words that calm and soothe, grunt words, snarls, guttural words, vocables and syllables, words like the sound of doves murmuring in immemorial elms, words crackling like fire, big sky words, cloud words, the clumsy words of first love, words like lucre, like treasure, wedding words, the keening words at gravesides, healing words,

words tumbling down in a waterfall of long golden hair, words you could climb, words turning a toad to a prince, Stonehenge words, words lost in the pit at Chichén Itzá, sweet Words run softly till I end my song, these words I have shored against my ruins, words I would kneel down before, all the way down, touching my forehead to the floor, words like a guillotine, unswerving, absolute, words to keep from going under, from breathing the dark waters, waiting words, maybe a ship will pass by, an island will rise up, maybe this will be the day I crawl ashore and you will see my wordprints in the sand leading toward the jungle—*there*—the fronds rustling, closing behind where I have disappeared into a new world, a luminous existence, a world so perfect there's no purpose for a poem, no need for words.

The Old Poets Home

What do you do if you're a poet and you come to that place where
there are no more poems, when the words are all used up for you,
when the Muse won't give you the time of day, or night, what do
you do, do you go to the Old Poets Home, sit around with Orpheus
and Homer and all the other silverbacks, Sappho in a bouffant blue-
gray wig sipping sherry, Eliot with his mouth like a prune, and what
do they do there, trade images, recall great lines, complain all day
how all the new poems seem so slick, so enameled, so gussied up,
so much *froufrou* and decoration, such silliness strutting around act-
ing important, or worse, confessions in the guise of poems, horrors,
details of the autopsy, poems like being run over by the ambulance,
and such little ambition, poems with no scale, no Vision, when will
there be a Major Poem they grouse, a Paradise Lost, an Intima-
tion of Immortality, look how they look with envy and contempt at
all the new metaphors cruising by in sleek metallic vehicles, boom
boxes throbbing with deep heavy basses, every now and then the
carriage of a sonnet creaking by, reminding them of the past, of the
glory that once was, how language lit up the dark night of the soul,
lit it up with suns and moonlight, with music and marvels, great vi-
sionary leaps, words falling like rain, like snow, like stars on fire,
but now here they all are, in the Old Poets Home, over there is old
blind Milton watching TV in his mind, and here comes Auden down
the hallway in a frayed robe, puffing a cigarette, face as crinkled as a
dried fig, and there's Whitman, beard down to his knees, still work-
ing the crossword of his Leaves, and there's Li Po trying to embrace
the moon in a fishbowl, and Emily upstairs peeking through her
keyhole, Longfellow wandering the halls in tears whispering *Re-
member me? Remember me?*, Donne proud and dressed in his shroud,

O what a sad and gloomy and forlorn place this is, but sometimes a few thoughtful, compassionate young poets will drop by with their groomed and friendly poems and let us stroke them, pet them, remember how once in our lives the poems frisked for us, barked, ran out ahead, full of energy and joy, looking back, tongue out, happy, looking back with eyes of love for their old masters, those kind and benevolent and sweet old poets.

Dolor

Sometimes in the quiet hours before dawn,
I lie awake, thinking of those other voices—
Tichborne in the Tower, pacing the night,
working his one poem before the absolute,
final day. Traherne's childlike voice,
lost for two hundred years, praising
a Lord of the common earth. Clare,
grieving his entire life over the loss
of Mary Joyce, walking thirty miles a day
with a sack of poems over his shoulder,
trying to interest anyone in his song.
And Keats coming out of the damp London night,
feverish, coughing into a white scarf—*I know
the color of this blood* brings the seasons
down on all of us.
     And I'm overcome
by the sorrow of it all. But grief is a place to begin,
a kind of clarity. Milton, exhausted and blind,
dictating to his churlish, petulant daughters,
began the Paradise at fifty-six.
And Hawthorne, twelve years alone in his room,
conjured dragons of the human heart,
perfecting the craft that would hold them
focused and brutal.
     In this quiet dark
I like to think of Emily, singing to herself,
as she looks out from her room

to the approaching carriage with its silent,
envious Driver, the horses' heads
turned toward Eternity, Emily singing
her way into the journey.

Homage to Night

I will give you
anything—light
against white
stone, stark wheat
fields of Kárpathos
in the pit of summer—
I will give you
everything—sapphire
of the Unicorn
tapestry, lapis and
carnelian—I will give
you rain over
the moors, violet
of owl's clover,
the green of green
fields—I will
give you taste,
cinnamon, music
and touch, O night
outside, night
within—radiant night,
night inside the rose
of day, keening
night, teeming river
of absence, obsidian
sea, night each night
growing larger, opening—

everything, all things
I am and have
I will give to you
O night coming, night
ahead—exacting,
severe, honest
night.

4

DAYBOOK, NIGHTBOOK: SHAY CREEK

Waking

These mornings
the Steller's jay comes to the railing outside my window,
comes with his impatient songs, his *rasps* and *burrs*, his news
of the new world, and I rise to greet him, I go out to the porch
and place on the rail a crust of bread, and the jay hops and squawks,
happy, I think, and me too when the mystery reveals itself, as it
does these mornings with *chirrs* and *sheks*, the best a jay
can do for singing, and good enough for me
as I wake and look out to the black-
crowned bolt of blue, alive
and squalling with
such brash
joy.

Lodestone

I lie in a hammock in the slow hours
of a summer day, summer at last
in the high country, summer in the air,
in the light, in the poems I'm reading,
poems like deep jade pools of snowmelt
under a summer sun, poems like
whorls of agate. There's a drift of pollen
through the forest, sifting through
the pines and cedars, a fine gold powder
drifting like the crushed ash of sunlight.
In the seep on the hillside the first
rein orchids appear, the night-blue larkspur,
leopard lilies. All summer the seep
will blaze with flowers under the flare
of sun over the Sierra. The day turns
around a single shaft of sunlight
through the pines. There's a whisper
of water from Shay Creek,
like the murmuring of voices
from far away, languorous voices,
honey-tongued, voices whispering
of summer, of stillness, the slow sound
of a heat-drowsed summer noon.
A warm wind rises up the canyon,
sways the pines. Clouds drift over.
If my body were the needle of a compass,

it would point dead center into the deep,
invisible lodestone of this murmuring,
immense, summer day.

In the Stream Pavilion

I walk
with Yang Wan-li out of the Sung dynasty
into the meadow below the hot springs.
We stop at Shay Creek, stand on the bank
and look down into a pool, a few trout
motionless in the shade, the water so clear
they hover in air. I tell Yang how I wish
my life were as translucent as Shay Creek,
how I want to follow it up the canyon
to its source, to the high snowfields above
the valley, above the lake, above everything,
up there in the keen air and blaze of sun.
Yang says, *I'm tired of walking. I want to*
lie down, take a nap. And no more poems
about rivers and mountains! He drops
a stone into the pool. *And the next time*
you're at this, put me in the imperial city,
or better yet, let me drink and be happy
like Li Po, drifting in a boat with only
the moon for company. I close my eyes.
When I open them — Yang is gone —
he's far downstream, where I've put him,
running the rapids standing in his boat,
shouting and laughing, drunk on wine.

Writing in Tongues

All things are holy! Blake claims,
but does that include these leeches,
these detached tongues squirming
in a pond near the hot springs?
If I stick my finger in the water
one of them will grope its way over
and wrap itself around a knuckle.
It has no eyes, has only a slit
for a mouth, has tiny, rasping teeth
that make a clean puncture, painless,
where it will feast on blood, swelling
with a leech happiness—but not
my blood! I slough the leech
from my finger, watch it squirm
back among its brethren, all of them
undulating in a kind of ecstasy, these
Holy Beings, these writhing tongues
of Blakean delight.

On What Planet

From Shay Creek, it's a two-hour drive:

- take Hot Springs Road to Markleeville, turn at the Cutthroat
- follow the East Fork of the Carson to the junction
- drive over Monitor and down into Slinkard
- then 395 south through Topaz to Walker
- go east—look for a dirt road coming out of the Sweetwaters
- drop into four-wheel drive
- take it slow, there are ruts and washouts, loose rocks, drop-offs
- when you reach a fork, take the right, ascending the canyon
- in two miles the road dead-ends at Desert Creek

If it's early summer, the banks of the creek will flame with larkspur
     and monkshood
By August they've withered and gone to seed
That's the time to come
Follow the creek a few miles back to its source, a small spring
     below the Sisters
And there you'll find them, in profusion—explorer's gentian
     (*Gentiana calycosa*), summer's last flowers
Go on, kneel down, get up close, peer into one
See how the blossom funnels into darker shades of blue,
     a cloister, speckled with light
It's like looking into a chalice flecked with stars
Then the mind will give a little nudge, and you are there,
     inside the singing, in a luminous alien night

During the Rains

Driving through the rain to Minden this morning, I saw two men walking in a lake that a week ago was pasture, two men ankle deep in the shallows, stringing barbed wire and trying to hammer fence posts into water, one holding a stake, the other with ferocity swinging a maul, horses standing around them, miserable, cattle up to their hocks in water, the Carson plain in flood, fields runneled with gills and freshets, culverts washed out, hillsides loosening, slipping, everything disintegrating, coming apart, the dead bear I found yesterday below Loope Canyon, skeleton unlocking, carcass sodden, dissolving in rain, and now this morning those two men near Minden driving stakes into water, stringing wire across a lake, trying to keep it all in, trying to keep it whole, driving these words into the page, as if this could make the bear stay, as if I could lash the body together, not let anything come apart, dissolve, wash away.

Over the Edge

When I step to the edge and look down, they're just getting out of the smashed pickup. She appears dazed, stunned, and he's trying to pull something out of the cab, gives up, and looks around. A heavy snow is falling. They begin a slow, awkward climb up the forty-foot slope. I start down toward them, kicking footholds in the ice. Half-way, I brace my feet, reach out my hand to his, and pull him up to me. He scrambles past. She's having difficulty. She can't make the few feet between us, so I edge down a little farther until our hands can grasp. But then I begin to slip, and for a moment I think we're both going to lose it, we're going to tumble to the bottom. But we don't. We clutch each other, then crab our way sideways to the top. The wind is blazing ice off the pass. Cars drift past in the blizzard, eerie faces behind glass peering out. I help the man and woman into my car. They don't say much. He has a gash on his forehead. But they're okay she insists. *We're okay.* You're lucky you're not dead, I'm thinking, wondering what they felt when they hit the ice and swerved over the edge. I crank the heater to high. The windows begin to fog. We're all breathing hard. I catch his eyes in the mirror. He looks away, ashamed, I think, the way he hurried up the slope without her. The woman turns in her seat. She's wiping the blood from his face. *We're going to make it,* she tells him. And we drive into the white heart of the storm.

Scatology

I'm climbing the trail up from Hangman's Bridge
heading into the hilly, open country below Leviathan.
Mostly scrub pine and sage. The dog runs out ahead,
her nose into everything. She halts. I come up
and look down. Old coyote scat. Marie looks around,
howls. We move on. Near the ridge, the earth's been
churned, and there's sheep dung everywhere, pellets
like desiccated *niçoise* olives. She sniffs a few.
Then we reach the head of the canyon and begin
a descent through rabbitbrush and dwarf piñon
to the east fork of the Carson. Suddenly Marie stops
before a mound, a heap, a small hill of bear shit,
still warm, full of berries with black seeds. She's
got her nose right down in it. She turns and stares
back at me with a glassy look, deranged by this
delicious new odor. I glance around, imagining
a bear somewhere near, maybe gazing at me,
or at Marie, who squats near the stack and adds
her own little hillock. Soon we're making tracks,
breaking a new trail down to the river, leaving
three mounds—still steaming—back in the canyon.

The Little Taj

Built the outhouse this summer—
Lundquist, master craftsman, came up
and we hammered it together—
cedar board-and-batten, pine interior,
window in the door facing up the canyon,
stained-glass window high on the back wall,
so when the morning sun shines through
it's like being inside a jewel—
got an oil heater, a bookshelf, footstool,
got one of those new composting toilets—
every six months gives you compost
pure enough to grow carrots in—
come on over and I'll sauté some
with fennel and a dribble of sage honey,
we'll sit on the porch with a glass of wine
and admire the outhouse—
you can see for yourself
why everyone's calling it the Taj Mahal,
best outhouse in all
of Alpine County.

Cutting Down the Jeffrey

Paul Hanning comes over with Bill Reese,
two chain saws, a can of gas, an ax, maul, some wedges,
and we all stand around and look up at the Jeffrey
towering next to the cabin, the Jeffrey that all winter
drops clumps of snow on the chimney, that sways
over the roof when the winds come up—so—
I've made up my mind to take it down, except
I'm not going to chainsaw a hundred-foot pine tree
and have it crash down and split my cabin in half—
so I hire Paul to come and do it. He squints up,
*Yup, that's a nasty lean. Where do you want me
to drop it?* I point up the hillside, an open space
between a cedar and some white fir. I figure
Paul's going to strap on his spikes and climb,
strip the limbs on the cabin side to shift the weight
of the fall, maybe even set a rope and have Bill
walk up the hillside with a come-along, but Paul
just eyeballs it. *How high you want the stump?*
Then jerks his big Stihl and begins the first cut.
I stand there with Bill, but I'm looking around
for which way I'm heading if this goes wrong.
Halfway through the trunk, Paul eases the bar out
and starts another cut, coming down at an angle,
and in five minutes he's sawed out a thick wedge,
looks like the slice of a watermelon. He walks
around to the cabin side and starts another cut.
Bill jams wedges into the crack, then sledges them

with the maul. The tree quivers, sways, there's a loud
crack, and the Jeffrey comes crushing down,
a huge leg-trembling jolt as it hits the mountainside,
exploding needles, resin and dust, branches
shattering into the air. And there's the tree
on the ground, dead center where I had pointed.
You want me to buck it? Paul asks, then walks
the trunk, whacking limbs with a two-bladed ax.
When he's bucked the tree into rounds,
we stand around, drinking a beer. *Where now?*
I ask Paul. *Up to Poor Boy. Beetles got a lot of trees*
up in there. Forest Service wants it thinned.
You need any cords after this, he laughs, *give a holler.*
When they leave, I gaze at the Jeffrey. It looks
like a shattered spine, like the broken back
of some creature from the Mesozoic, vertebrae
strewn over the hillside. Now no more clumps
of snow on the chimney, no more waking at night
in windstorms waiting to be crushed. Now
there's firewood for two winters, and there's
woodsplitting to be done, the stacking of woodpiles,
there's morning after morning of work to do.
I look at the stump, the shimmering of air above it,
the emptiness, the ghostly absence of what once
was there. The Jeffrey, the great old Jeffrey,
is down.

Taste and See

Walking the trail to the waterfall, I decide to take a new route, and soon I'm in an old conifer forest, when I see them, crowning through duff and needles, a group of mushrooms. Back at the cabin, I take Arora from the shelf, and key them: brown cap, white gills, rosy blush to the flesh, partial veil. So. Probably Blushers (*Amanita rubescens*), usually edible if cooked, but poisonous raw. "Not recommended," Arora says. And besides, they're amanitas, family of the Destroying Angel (*Amanita ocreata*). Arora advises, "Better to be safe than sorry." But look at them, spread out on the table, fresh from the earth, delicate gills, stalks the color of salmon flesh, odor of storms and autumn. What would they taste like? What if I sauté a few in butter, with shallots, a dash of *fumé blanc*, black pepper. Then sit down and wait for the blush. Put on some music, something Tibetan, Gyuto monks chanting the Mahakala sadhana. Lie back and listen. Wait for the quickening pulse, fever, delirium, visualizing Mahakala, demonic lord of wrath and transcendence, with his six arms, his dagger, his necklace of skulls. I could do this. I could see the world within this world. I could invite danger into my life. Look at them, amanitas, rubescent little blushers. I could spin the wheel, step out on the edge. I could taste. And see.

Sierra Bardo

You're hiking Thunder Ridge into one of those dark, red fir forests, the trees all crowded together, half of them dead or dying, moss hanging from limbs. There's a drizzle of rain, a gloom-filled day. The dog runs ahead, runs back, barking. You work your way up under the ridge, jagged cliffs with caves high up, and you're thinking you could be in Dolpo or Mustang, Milarepa's world, monks in caves chanting ecstatic poems. Then you skirt the ridge and start down, following a dry streambed, wildflowers all withered, gone to seed. Crossing over an old logging road, you hear a sound, far off, sounds like some idiot with a chain saw, but this far into the forest? The snarling gets louder, and before you can understand, you see a man in black leathers on a dirt bike crashing down the road, and behind him another, and a moment later, another, all wearing dirt masks, armor, crash helmets, their 250 cc Yamahas thrashing past as you stand off the road, stunned. And then they are gone, leaving a sound trailing off, exhaust fumes thinning into the firs, and you feel as if you've entered the Bardo, the dead time between worlds, feel as if no matter where you go, even 9,000 feet in the high country, the Nightmare will manifest, will come down, will claim you.

Homage to the Presence of the Mystery Among Us

All afternoon on the hillside above the hot springs,
dozing and reading, in the July heat, looking now
and then across the ravine to the large boulders
and mottled shade, not paying much attention,
just drowsing, drifting, daydreaming, letting
the scene wash over me without focusing,
without noticing until later that night,
staring into the fire, into the Roman
world of flames and ember, when
it came to me, that shape on the
ravine side, in the shadows,
where I had been so long
in gazing—and where
finally now I see the
great antlered head
turn and the buck
rise to its feet
& disappear
into the
deeper
shade
of
day

Wintering

October 11—
Woke this morning to snowfall,
kindled a fire in the woodstove,
made coffee, looked out the window
to white trees and silence. Today
I'll do little. Maybe read a few Masters
from the Sung dynasty, maybe work
on the poem that's been eluding me.
Yesterday I stacked firewood—
incense cedar, Jeffrey, white fir—
lugging them up from the woodpile,
stacking a cord chest high on the porch.
Around noon the weather turned,
clouds streaming in from the west,
and now this morning the first snow.
Yang says, *The mountains are chilled
by a cold sun. Autumn light trickles
into my poem.* I think of the winter
to come, how the sun will walk the ridge,
how light will scale the canyon.
In those months, sealed in,
I'll build fires in the woodstove,
watch the logs seethe to embers.
All winter I'll let the poem burn
within me, tempering each word
in silence, in the winter sun
forging my life, honing my spirit
in the country of light.

Homage to the Thief

In snowshoes,
pulling a sled loaded with gear,
I plod my way up to the cabin
and find the door
broken in, a foot of snow
drifting into the kitchen.
A black bear? — that old bachelor
that hung around the canyon
last fall? But a bear with a taste
for Tennessee bourbon,
the whole bottle empty, the top
carefully unscrewed, next to a shot glass
on the kitchen table? And my
buck knife's gone, my compass,
my book of Weston nudes.
Well now. Buddha says
we don't own anything. He's right,
of course, we don't even own
these bodies that walk us over snow,
that break in doors, crumple
pages of poems to build
a fire. There are some who claim
we get to come back in another
body, get to keep coming back
until we get it right. What would
this thief return as? A jackal?
And given my life, what about me?
An ox? A bumblebee?

Dear Thief, thank you
for cutting me loose,
thank you for these thoughts.
Maybe now I'll try to live
another kind of life, maybe I'll even
get lucky, I'll get to come back
as an egret, solitary, standing
long hours in fields, gazing into pools,
no doors, owning nothing, standing
under open sky, now raising
my wings, rising above the river,
flying over the fields at dusk,
now disappearing
into night.

Drinking Wine with T'ao Ch'ien, Looking into the Fire

All November
I've been living with T'ao Ch'ien,
who has been teaching me
idleness and drinking as the Way.
For idleness, T'ao says,
you must visualize its character:
moonlight shining
through an open door.
I'm a willing student,
but the legend of Yen Hui
troubles me: Hui who mastered idleness
so perfectly, he refused to eat,
and starved. Confucius said,
Hui has made it. He is empty.
But I say, that's a bit extreme.
What about the Middle Way, the Golden Mean?
T'ao Ch'ien smiles, tells me
to put more wood in the stove.
Let go and forget it all, he says.
Life soon returns to nothing.
I feed chunks of cedar into the old Jøtul.
Let's have some wine to warm us up,
make us feel a little immortal.
So we drink, and gaze into the fire —
we see flaring cities, spirits of dead friends,

we see the dancing shapes of the Way,
the beginning of all philosophy,
and its end. *Let's live this day in joy,*
it isn't tomorrow we're looking for.
T'ao pours more wine. Outside
snow sifts down in a white ash.
T'ao says, *A thousand years are beyond us,*
but this moment we can turn into forever.

Living Alone

Loveliest of what I leave behind
is the sunlight
and loveliest after that the shining stars
and the moon's face
but also cucumbers that are ripe
and pears and apples

PRAXILLA OF SIKYON
(CA. 450 B.C.)

This morning Praxilla asks me if I know
Han-shan, if I have ever been to Cold Mountain,
do I know the way, could I take her there.
I tell her—this is Shay Creek, we're 6,000 feet
in the Sierra Nevada—in the dead of winter.
Why do you want to leave Sikyon, where pears
ripen in the sun? Why make that long climb
out of the classical world, to follow a trail
disappearing among cliffs and clouds? Even
if you're lucky and able to find Han-shan,
he's just a cranky old hermit who won't say
anything, probably won't even invite you
to sit down. Praxilla sighs. It's hard to live
in this one poem, she says, even if it is full
of sunlight and stars. When you close the book,
I have no other life. So open Han-shan, put me
on Cold Mountain. Besides, you have nothing
better to do, and it's been snowing for days—
you can go with me, we'll both visit Han-shan,

and I bet he'll welcome us, we'll sit and gaze
into his fire, we'll drink green tea, he's been
on that mountain for so long, he too must tire
of living alone, must miss human company.

Reading Joyce in Winter

I sit in bed reading "The Dead"
the night of winter solstice
I'm on this side of the world
this side of the seasons
my spirit waiting for dawn to open
the slow-opening morning glories
I planted with seeds of fire
before I came to this mountain
before I entered winter
and its days going out like embers
the silence so huge
I can hear snow falling over the Spur
over Burnside and the Hawk
falling across my life
filling the hours the days
where someday I will become
one of the shades
the snow drifting out of the night
lit by the moon as if all the stars
were coming down on fire
drifting through the pines
and falling across Shay Creek
across the Bog of Allen falling
into the dark mutinous Shannon waves
flake by flake the snow
falling faintly through the night

softly falling like the descent
of the last end upon all
the living and the dead

Late Night, Year's End, Doing the Books with Tu Fu

for Sam Hamill

Ghost fires in the jade palace. Moonlight
a scattering of opals on the river. Over us
beasts of the zodiac march across the night.
We drink cup after cup of warm rice wine.
It's time to take out the ledger, to figure
the year's accounts. Tu Fu, if our days
and nights are the principal, if all the years
are interest, then how much do we owe?
If I subtract my grief from joy, what is left?
Tell me, old friend, how does it balance?
In one of your last poems you talk about
the stars outside your hut, how impossible
to count them. *There are no numbers,*
you say, *for this life. Who cares if we're
in the red? Or the black? Add a few zeros,
and we're rich. Erase a few, and we're poor.*
You're right, Tu Fu. Rich or poor, the night
each night burgeons within us. The mornings
open with sunlight. Why count them?
Instead of numbers, let me enter words
into the ledger, this account of our friendship,
this little poem from me to you, across
the glimmering, innumerable years.

Homage: Summer/Winter, Shay Creek

IN THE SHINING

I've got my chair and a good book and I'm sitting
out behind the cabin in a shaft of sunlight, reading.
A couple of Steller's jays who might be my friends
perch themselves on branches in the ponderosa
and sugar pine. They can't read the book I've got
but they can read me, and they watch very carefully
for that moment when my hand reaches in-
to my pocket and pulls out some crusts of bread
which I toss out over the forest floor and the jays
spring off the limbs and streak down in a blue blaze,
scoop the crusts and are back in the limbs again
chortling. This is the way of my life these days—
lazing, serene, but not so indolent, not so torpid
that I won't get up now and then, grab my chair,
and move to another spot, over there by the cedar,
to that new place shining now in the sun.

MANNA

Everywhere, *everywhere*, snow sifting down,
a world becoming white, no more sounds,
no longer possible to find the heart of the day,
the sun is gone, the sky is nowhere, and of all
I wanted in life — so be it — whatever it is
that brought me here, chance, fortune, whatever
blessing each flake of snow is the hint of, I am
grateful, I bear witness, I hold out my arms,
palms up, I know it is impossible to hold
for long what we love of the world, but look
at me, is it foolish, shameful, arrogant to say this,
see how the snow drifts down, look how happy
I am.

ALL THE ROOMS ARE BURNING

The Singing, the Darkness,
the Earth as Language

But how to accommodate death?
Tsang-kie invented writing, it is said,
by observing bird tracks around the lake.
From their prints he could tell what songs
had been there. But the night birds
leave no tracks. The owl under the sickle moon
glides silent through the dark, touches down
only to seize its prey. We know its home
from the droppings of skulls,
pellets of fur and bone.

Lupine

I came into the years
with you, mother,
and now I must endure the silence
of these early, February flowers.

⁓

Death like rain
washes us clean.
Mother, is it so?

⁓

Mother, no
word of mine
shall find you.

Lament

after Lorca

Because the moon became my mother
No need to weep
Because the tree broke open its honey
No need to weep
Because the blade *always* finds the heart
No need to weep

To Han-shan

I

Often in this life
I think of you—
marriage broken, sick of the world,
making the treacherous journey
to Cold Mountain.
You came closer than any of us
to stone, stream, cloud.
To the pearl of the mind.
Thirty years alone with silence,
cliffs,
your laughter and tears.
The Governor who expected wisdom
sent his aides ahead
bearing gifts and medicine.
O Han-shan,
screaming "Thieves! Thieves!"
before you disappeared
                      into the mountain.

2

I've come to the age
when you abandoned everything—
wife, home, and friends—
to begin the solitude of Cold Mountain.
I've come all these years to this
ignorance, this failure
to complete even the simplest of things.
Each day I begin.
By night I am stunned back
to the empty page,
while others, casually,
build their house.
I come finally to the orchard,
drunk and naked in the rain
being led home by a girl.
Cold Mountain
Cold Mountain
is inside me.

Calligraphy

In Calgary
I saw a man break a dog's back.
Leaves on a white hill.
The moment as ideogram
I cannot translate.
The absolute, actual tree
shames my life.
And Pound singing how splendid the words,
like marble,
persist through time.
Virtù in the vortex of death.
Calligraphy of what the seasons leave
to the mind.
The city in the heart
in ruins.
The dog broken in the street.
White hill.
Leaves.

Grief

Went to the Wailing Wall of the Jerusalem within me.
My father was there, weeping. My mother was there, wailing
and weeping. The little boy I was, sobbing and pleading.
The prophet was there, predicting ruin, the falling of mountains.
The walls of the city, the portals of the body, collapsing.
Went weeping to the Wall of the death of my brother's daughter.
Stood in the courtyard among the moneychangers
listening to the sound of coins changing hands,
the city everywhere around me in flames, the graves
open, Apocalypse coming down, and rain like a black fire.

Notes Toward a 19th-century Painting

Begin with light—
the water a silvery gray against the far shore,
a glassy green in the major body edged with ebony,
late-afternoon mist blurring the shape of distant fir,
the sleek back of a whale barely visible in the channel.
In the lower foreground an island emerges,
then a cabin tilting above shoreline on a croppage of rocks.
Three figures stand around a cairn—
two men and a woman, their postures discrete, private.
One, his back to us, drunk, stares out toward the whale.
The woman, slightly apart, with sharp almost Indian features,
gazes furiously at some place far and cold within her.
The last figure, eyes attentive to his hands, sharpens an ax.
The clouded sky swirls, textured like marble.
On the horizon, volcanic peaks. Beyond them, emptiness.
How small the figures appear in the painting.
How persistently the perspective sweeps our eyes back to them,
hesitating, suggesting something about to happen,
as if someone were going to step out of the silence,
as if there were something to say.

Death in the Tehachapis

Mr. Cox would fall asleep in the armchair still gripping
his drink. He'd doze awhile, come to, take a sip, then
drift off again. Someone stoked wood in the fireplace.
Hunters came in with shotguns and dead quail. Then
a smell of coffee and potatoes frying in a black skillet.
Mr. Cox waking and nodding, weaving in and out of it,
clutching his drink, the one he invented, a glass of gin
and crushed ice topped with burgundy, the wine
drifting down like a thick cloud the color of blood.
Outside, a vicious Tehachapi wind. A poker game inside,
money on the table, half a dozen men playing for keeps,
now and then someone gazing toward the armchair,
the anchor of that room, the polestar, hunters and hunted,
Death stalking slowly, spectral, coming in for the kill.

City

Of course the heart is nothing
but muscle and blood, a chambered organ
the size of your fist, prone to attack
and failure. We can't include it
in modern poems, having given up
that old cadence for this slaughtered prose.
Once the heart was like a city,
medieval, the cobbled streets led down
to the slums near the river. At night
thieves were about. There's a butcher shop
by the stable where in the morning you can hear
the high screams of pigs as they are hung
by their hocks and their throats slit.
It's snowing now, and a crowd gathers
around the gallows as the Bishop in his gold robe
forgives a sinner in the name of a greater King
than the one in the castle on the hill, who sits
among his tapestries, alone and afraid.
Far off you can hear the airs of a minstrel
singing *timor mortis conturbat me.*
And there are rumors going around:
of glass which magnifies the face in the moon,
of wondrous, far-off lands, cities made of gold,
talking beasts, the rare unicorn. But here
the peasants are hungry, revolt is in the air.
An old man in a cluttered, upper room of the city
sits at his desk and turns in his hands

the shriveled, toadlike remains of a human heart,
and begins to calculate through reason alone
how everything in God's earth, or heaven,
can be known.

Waiting for the Barbarians

The old man in the café could have been Cavafy—
the way the cup trembled in his hand, the ardor
in his eyes behind thick glasses, his furtive glances
toward the young man. The old poet looked
so out of place sitting among ferns and oak furniture,
Coltrane's *A Love Supreme* smoldering from speakers.
The young man sat across from me, long ponytail,
a diamond in his earlobe, dour mouth.
                                    I moved
my queen across the board, through a landscape littered
with knights and pawns. I thought of the ancient city
of Alexandria, a room above the Arab quarter, a man
imagining his life as a series of candles—a few up ahead
lit and shining, an army strung out behind, burnt down,
wisps of smoke curling like incense into the room.
The man sits there conjuring his youth when Eros
ruled all his blood.
                    Cavafy, I know you're just a shade
in the underworld of language. All day I've been sitting here,
waiting for moves, for insight on how to proceed. The old man
still looks our way, but he is bored and tired. Coltrane's fire
has been returned to silence. Across from me
the young man keeps raising his head, his face sullen, eyes
without expression, as game after game we isolate, humiliate,
and murder our kings.

Interlude: To an Audience

I want to write a poem
that will embody in you something
alien. A crow, for instance,
clutching the branch of a dead oak
in a dry riverbed five miles outside
of Hollister. A sleek, sharp bird,
eyeing the heap of bones that was once a cow.
I would have you in that tree all day,
with the sun in its long, slow arc
turning the fields into flames of weeds,
seedpods cracking in the heat,
the chattering sparrows nervous
under your gaze. I want you
to observe in the distance a man
stalking through milkweed and thistle.
He'll stop a hundred feet away, wipe
his brow with a sleeve, and swing the rifle
to his shoulder. I want you to look
into that barrel a long time, before
the quick sunburst and shattering
of branches, as you wing from the limb,
and fly, cawing and cursing, over the sprawling,
logical suburbs.

On the Rib-bone of a Cow

Where the river went dry
this rib
      stark white
            in a bed of white stones

—————

In the gradual curve
          of the rib
the lucid architecture of death

—————

Inside the hard bone
the marrow is honeycombed
            Small, secret chambers
of dark bees, death's honey

—————

The Angels, splendid
        in their white flames,
fail
    before the elemental touch
          of bone

Of the Body

I. SHINE

I climbed the ladder into the spring morning
and stood swaying among bees blazing in honeysuckle,
my pruning shears butchering vines so rank they bent
the trellis. Stretching, I balanced on the ladder, reaching out
over the edge, into the flames of honeysuckle, cottonwood
shimmering a green fire, leaning into a slow motion
of shears thudding to the deck, the ladder away from me
going over—and the bottom dropped out—body
flailing, I watched myself fall, watched as my arm stiffened
to brace body weight, palm smacking the wood deck,
a shock of force jolting my arm out of its socket—
I writhed on the deck, guttering and retching, my arm
a grotesque angle from its shoulder—then
the slow drive to the hospital, all things in rapture,
a paraclete of tongues, the nurse's face suffused with light,
pain grinding me back into my life, past sorrow, back
into the blood hum of my body, into the dragon shine.

2. SEIZURE

Dawn in the San Joaquin, I get out of the car
to stretch and let the dog romp awhile in a field
when my body suddenly begins to stutter, quake
uncontrollably, and part of me watches, detached,
thinking—*is this a heart attack? a stroke?*—
as my trunk and limbs buck and flail and I
keel onto my back, convulsing. After a time
I see the dog across the field chasing something
and who I am comes back to my body
which has quieted, and I lie on the ground,
cheek against the earth, my ear listening to a pulse
from the underworld that gradually becomes
my heart. I pull myself up, hold on to the car door
as the dog trots over, tongue out, happy—and me, too,
happy to be in this field below the Gold Country,
a moment in spring, in the 53rd year of my life,
wondering what it was that broke open the morning,
scattering incandescence everywhere, the trees
across the way still pulsing, shimmering as if in flames,
and within my body a hushed feeling, beatitude,
a silence closing around silence.

Venom

I

It had to happen, it *has* to happen.
This time it was Steve.
The doctor said *melanoma*
and all the doors into the bright mornings
began slamming shut.
I remember how embarrassed he was, *I* was,
when we met on the path coming up from the bunkhouse.
A summer day, the garden going crazy with squash and beans,
the cornstalks a green Gauguin never found in paradise.
I remember our eyes met quickly,
quickly looked away,
to the garden, to the ground, to the seeping faucet,
the slick shine of water disappearing,
soaking into the earth.
Well, he said.
And months later in an Indian ashram
seeking a miracle,
Steve,
someone told me this,
pointed to the photo of the guru on the wall,
—accusation? recognition?—
pointed his finger at it,
as if there were something profound in the gesture,

something outside language,
beyond meaning,
and his life just
left him.

2

It was the way the skunk looked at me
after my dog mauled it
the night it tried to raid the chicken hutch.
I was in the kitchen, reading,
when the night tore itself apart.
I rushed outside—
the dog whimpered around the yard,
scrubbing her face on the ground.
Then I saw the skunk, struggling to move,
dragging its hind legs.
When I approached, it stopped,
looked up at me.
The whole yard smelled of burnt rubber.
Holy Christ, I muttered.
It continued to look at me,
no pleading, no anger,
no fear on its face.
One dying creature
looking at another.
I knew I had to do something—
half its guts trailed from its belly.
I got the shovel, the new one,
and held the tip above the skunk's neck.
It continued to stare.
I thrust down, trying to sever the head.
It took three blows.
The dog rubbed against my leg.

Sad, angry, disgusted,
I gave a swift kick,
missed,
and stood leaning against the shovel
wondering what do I do now,
what's next,
what do I do with this mess,
this body.
The dog yowled, whined,
unable to rid the smell from her muzzle.
I called to her,
held out my hand, touched her head,
calmed her.
Then walked to the corner of the yard
where the limbs of the pear tree,
heavy with fruit,
bent down almost to the ground.
I stuck the blade of the shovel into the earth
and began to dig.

Midterm, between *Hamlet* and *Heart of Darkness*, First Day of Our Bombing in Afghanistan

'Tis bitter cold, and I am sick at heart.
               I leave the class
writing on a passage in *Hamlet*—they can work it out
for themselves—and walk the hillside above campus
brooding over graves standing tenantless, the dead
gibbering in the streets under stars with trains of fire
and dews of blood, disasters in the sun and in the skies
above Jalalabad, where today the world broke open,
where I once sat by the road and broke open a sweet melon
after months of travel—across the Punjab, to Lahore,
over Khyber Pass, then down to the orchards
and melon fields of Jalalabad. Thirty years ago.
From this hill I look out over Monterey Bay, storm clouds
backlit by the sun, looking like a world on fire,
or like a great dragon torn apart, its black pearl
clutched in a talon of the sun. What are my students
making of Hamlet's dilemma—*to be, or not to be?*
Do they think it's simply rhetoric? Grist for a test?
Do they know it will become their own question?

                          Poor Shakespeare,
writing with the ink of his blood after the death
of Hamnet, his only son. Is it true there is a divinity
that shapes our ends? Our president thinks so.
The Taliban think so. And Hamlet, it appears,
came to believe it. But the others, those who work
to grow melons, work to put food into the mouths
of children — what shapes their ends through the years,
years of fear and slaughter, famine and horror?
How do they endure the wars of Enduring Freedom?
I tell my students *Hamlet* is a classic revenge play —
what would *you* do to avenge your father's murder?
Laertes would slit a throat in church, he would risk
the loss of both worlds. We woke one morning
and the towers were falling. We woke to terror
and the murder of our brethern. And today we begin
our revenge — the stage littered with corpses,
the deaths of fathers, of sons and daughters, mothers.
And the curtain will not come down — the audience
will not applaud — busy as we are
cutting each other's throats.
                          It is bitter cold
in a bitter world, and I am sick at heart. All down
the coastal range creeks are flowing into the sea.
Out there under the Pacific the grey whales
make their passage. I imagine Hamlet walking
inside the enormous skull of a whale — what then
would be the shape of his thoughts? Poor Yorick.
Poor clown. Poor fools grappling in an open grave
over the corpse of Ophelia. For what? Love? Honor?
On the hillside where I walk, I see emerging

from earth the tiny, spear-shaped skulls of morels.
I used to think of them as the shape of flames,
dark flowers burning out of the shades, flowers
of that undiscovered country from where no traveler
returns. But that's a Hamlet thought. I *have* lived
his question. I have made my own answer. I bear it
with me as I walk back thinking of beginnings. Of ends.
Soon the class will begin another journey, with Marlow,
going up a river like traveling back to the beginnings
of this world. Will Marlow show us the source
of the horror? Will Kurtz? I look out to sea,
the far horizon under a bank of clouds, a waterway
leading to the uttermost ends of the earth, somber
under a darkening sky, ribbons of light unraveling,
disappearing into the heart of an immense darkness.

Bible

The spider crab exults: *Look at me! I, too, am of the glory
of this world.* A field mouse turns to the snake: *This
is my body. This is my blood.* The scorpion scuttling
from under a rock, arms wide, pincers open, wants
to embrace us—it has news, friends—the tip
of its tail bears a psalm from Isaiah. And the heron
is Lord of the Apocalypse stalking across the pool,
choosing and stabbing: *This one. That one.*
My chosen ones.

Letter to Rachel, Seattle, Summer 1973

The whole wall was luminous and hung with negatives.
I could see the perfect, elegant bones shining
and the skull grin under the flesh
as the doctor traced his finger along the thin line
of fracture.
             I remembered how the motorcycle
couldn't turn the corner, the slow buckling
of the wheel as I went over the handles.
On the way to the hospital I thought of you,
and as the doctor worked over my face—
the quick, painless puncture of the needle,
his detached hands threading and sewing
as he hummed and talked of how our body
is simply water's
                most intricate
catch, its most complex vehicle for traveling
over the earth—I was thinking how fragile
the body is,
           how fine
those quiet mornings to wake and listen
to your breathing—the other miracle, that flesh
could catch
           this love, however brief
or broken.

Lines

I wasn't about to believe her—this seer, this psychic—

and wondered what she would say as she read the lines
in my palm. I didn't want to know about my future—
I was still puzzling over the past—the future seemed
obvious, a fierce ravenous engine railing around the bend.
The seer, drunk under the winter night, squinted

over my open palm, and I admit it shook a little,
a slight tremble, nothing much. I could feel
my heart pump the blood down through my arm.
I tried to resist this miracle, tried not to be obvious
about my own gaze at the arm of the psychic—

the needle marks, the tracks in the veins in the soft
crease of skin above her forearm. I was thinking
maybe she should try her skill at reading those lines—
how far into the future *they* led. She worked
at a crisis center, eight years answering a phone

and counseling the lonely, the drunks, the suicidal
who wanted a witness, who didn't want to die alone—
The memory and horror of one call, silence on the line,
then the *crack* of a pistol.
Her gift was well known—police consulted her

for clues to murders—perhaps she could envision
where the body of the little boy might be,
In the bushes down the ravine outside Boulder Creek.
But she never got it quite right—she was accurate
about the fire road and the manzanita brush—

but the body was in the next county. So I wasn't
greatly worried as she began to trace my lines—
how this one meant I had lived a rich life, and where
this one forked meant someone close to me had died
and a part of me had died also, and this jagged line, this scar

cutting across the others—*This one is the love line*—
You've been lucky, you've had a great love in your life—
See here, how the line leaves the palm, traces
the air, how it zigs and zags, rising, seeking,
rises toward the sharp points of stars,

crosses the zodiac, connecting planets and nebulae
into the shapes of beasts drifting across night—*an amazing love*—
And she's weeping now, holding my palm, squeezing it,
hard, clutching and talking about love, how she can't see
where it's going, where it ends, and I'm sitting there,

dumbly, looking at her, wondering about this, not so much
interested in where it's going, or where it's been, but where
is it—what's it doing in my life, in hers—and suddenly
I begin to believe she might be right—how it's here,
now, right *here*, in the clasping, sweating, scarred

palms of our hands, bridged together, holding on.

Sky Diving

A morning in autumn, years ago. I was living out back in the shed, the
pony barn we called it, a simple whitewashed room full of windows,
with a bed, woodstove, bookshelves, a desk. I was in bed looking up
through the skylight, past the bare branches of the walnut trees, into
the sky where a group of seagulls rode a thermal in a huge rotating
gyre. I was thinking about the skydiver with a camera strapped to
him, a filmmaker, who the week before leaped after a group of div-
ers who had formed a great circle in the sky—which he plunged into,
spinning the camera around. The TV news had shown the footage.
I was thinking of this when Sarah called out my name and walked
into the shed. I can still see her, standing there, blue jeans and san-
dals, white T-shirt, her hair damp from a shower, smelling of bal-
sam and resin. She had recently returned from Germany, leaving her
husband, beginning the divorce, the ugly struggle. She stood there,
hesitant, embarrassed, saying the words she must have rehearsed.
I could not cross over. I couldn't even manage the dignity of a *no*. I
just let the moment move into the larger day, into the season and the
years that have brought me here. I let her stand there to make small
talk, to listen as I told her about the news program, how the divers
broke off from their circle, doing backflips, tumbles, a crude aerial
ballet. And then the part in the film where their chutes unravel and
they are suddenly jerked up out of sight while the camera continues
to record—the wobbling horizon, ground enlarging from below,
the landscape beginning to swing crazily—and you realize some-
thing's wrong, the cameraman is out of control. On the morning
of the jump, amid the crowd and confusion, he hadn't been paying
attention, distracted, thinking maybe of his cameras and lenses, and

didn't put on his chute, which he realized only when he reached for the cord. And there I was talking away, wondering aloud what his thoughts were those last moments plunging into the uprushing ground—while Sarah stood there, the expression on her face looking at me—our own time and terror crashing down with us as we hurtled to earth.

Book of Horror

Look at the garden
look at the honeysuckle
burned black
by the freeze
look how everything green
has been torched
look at the sheath of ice
over the pond
the ghost flames of goldfish
streaking embers of sun
little memories
of how this garden once
seethed with cosmos iris foxglove
now look
a death camp of dead flowers
in one night the killer freeze
like a wrecking ball through a rose window
blossoms
shattered into ice
as if Yamantaka
the Bodhisattva of Wrath
had come down among us
plundering and ravaging

sheathing everything in frost
giving us a glimpse
of the glacial world ahead
an ice planet
drifting around a dead
burned-out star

WHAT GOT ME

I'll tell you what got me
in the Solomon Islands
up in the jungle past
the chanting and dancing
beyond the rusted hulks of tanks
sunk to their turrets in seawater
past the man selling mango ice cream
from a wooden bucket
way up there where air turns to mist
and leaves drip and smell like poison
where little demons scuttle
out of holes in the mud
with eyes on stalks and hold out
one huge claw
like a club
their carapace the color of the inside
of orchids hanging
like ghost fires among the branches

up there amid the flesh smell
of corpse flowers
among the fox bats and bushpigs
among ground vipers the color of ground
geckos that sound like frogs
frogs that sound like dogs
insects the shape of leaves and sticks
ants pouring out of a crack in the earth
as if fleeing from some terror
all this seething steaming life
everywhere over everything
swarming beside me around me
brother I tell you that's
what got me

PAIN

The pain
was too great
for my body
so they slipped me
through a needle
then I was
nowhere
and when I came to
my body was wrapped
as for burial

the light around me
from no source
a man
wearing a mask
stood over me
saying
all has been accomplished
he touched me
from across
an empire
burning
with cones of fire
where a white
gauze of ash
drifted
over the pyre
that was my
body

Question and Answers

Why did you do it?

Because of those topaz mornings

Because of the weeping inside the marriage

Because of the fire and the rain and the fire

Because of the night train from Singapore to Kuala Lumpur

Because the peach, the spoon, the bowl, the cream, the sugar

Because my teachers were *pain* and *desire* and *almost*

Because of lions and gold and pearls in the wheat

Because the dog in my dream was the dog in my yard

Because my father turned in the doorway and looked back at me

Because of empire, silk sheets, cheap perfume, coins

Because of the great night over me each night

Because the monk sat there, serene, back straight, as his body
    went up in flames

Because the mynah bird kept repeating *You want me to* H U RT *you?*

Because Ellen's chicken walked into my kitchen looking me over
    with its only eye

Because the panther tattooed on the biceps will rise in that other
    kingdom someday

The Death of Lorca

Because you have died forever,
like all the dead of the Earth,
like all the dead who are forgotten
in a heap of lifeless dogs.

FEDERICO GARCÍA LORCA

The Black Squad of the Falangists arrested Lorca. They took him from Granada to Víznar in the Sierra de Alfacar. He spent the night in the Villa Concha. By then he knew he was to be executed in the morning. He wanted Confession, but the priest, who attended the other prisoners, had already left. The guard, José Jover Tripaldi, told the terrified poet — *If you ask God's forgiveness, your sins will be forgiven.* Lorca could only remember parts of prayers, a few phrases from his childhood. At dawn, a schoolteacher, two anarchist bullfighters, and Lorca were walked toward the Fuente Grande. They could hear the sound of water from the spring the Arabs called Ainadamar — the Fountain of Tears. Lorca knew by heart the medieval poem of Abū'l-Barakāt al Balafīqī —

> *At Ainadamar the birds sing*
> *as great as musicians*
> *in the Sultan's court.*
> *Their song opens in me*
> *that place I entered in my youth,*
> *where the women,*
> *the moons of that world,*
> *beautiful as Joseph,*

made every Believer
abandon his faith
for love.

The four men were shot beside an olive grove. Lorca did not die from the first fusillade. He had to be finished with a coup de grâce. Juan Luis Trescastro boasted in a taverna that he had been part of the squad, that he had finished Lorca off—*with two bullets in the ass for being queer.* An hour after the executions, the gravedigger arrived. He recognized the two bullfighters, observed that the third man had a wooden leg, and the fourth wore a loose tie—*you know, the sort that artists wear.* He buried the bodies in a trench, one on top of another, in no particular order.

Rune

after the Anglo-Saxon

Traveler

    stop

before this stone

    with its honeycomb

under the earth

    Take warning

Don't be

    too happy

The odor will rise

    the Furies will

smell it

    will be on you

like bees

    Of your joy

they'll make

    their honey

as they did

    of mine

in my summer

    my time

in the place

    where you

now stand

Stitching the Woe Shirt

in memoriam:
Kelly Stroud

Inconsolable

ॐ

As if a word could name it

ॐ

As if sorrow were an ax

ॐ

As if a prophet opening the body could read the future

ॐ

As if a god reached in and scattered her across time

ॐ

Inconsolable

ॐ

As if *grief* and *anguish* and *desolation* were threads

ॐ

As if this poem were a needle

Elsewhere

My father picks up my brothers and me at the swimming pool. He is angry and smells of gin. We get in the car. No one speaks. He drives back to the wedding party to get my mother. An aunt takes me aside, puts her hands on my shoulders — "Your father is a good man. Remember this. Sometimes we don't mean to do the things we do." In the car, my mother sits up front. Against her cheek she holds a towel wrapped around ice. We drive across the hot L.A. Basin. We are on the freeway, among the other cars with families inside. We are all driving, from somewhere, to somewhere else.

᠂ᡃ

I pick up the phone and it's a woman's voice. She wants to speak with my father. I go back to the dinner table. My brothers drink their milk. My mother looks at her plate. I wait for my father to come back. Our dog is asleep under the table. His name is *Fury*. When my father sits down, he's wearing a face. We go back to eating. Then we're in the den. With our first TV. We all sit before it. No one gets up to change to a new channel. From the night outside, our window glows like a screen. If you were to look in, you would see what appears to be a family.

Knots

Trying to tie my shoes, clumsy, not able to work out
the logic of it, fumbling, as my father stands there,
his anger growing over a son who can't even do
this simplest thing for the first time, can't even manage
the knot to keep his shoes on—*You think someone's
going to tie your shoes for you the rest of your life?*—
No, I answer, forty-five years later, tying my shoe,
hands trembling with this memory. My father
and all those years of childhood not being able to work out
how he loved me, a knot so tight it has taken all my life
to untie.

A Story from the Fifties

This is about the family who lived down the street. The husband — in the yard on weekends, pruning, mowing the lawn, raking, the usual. The son — a quiet boy, who kept to himself. The mother we rarely saw; she stayed mostly inside the house. This was back when there were housewives, when after the husbands went to work and the kids were off to school, the neighborhood came alive with women. Visits, phone calls, coffee-chats, all weaving through housework, errands, the tending of babies. But this mother, this wife, did not visit, did not chat. Some said she began her mornings with those stubby cans of Country Club Malt. And by noon would be pickled. *Pickled.* That was the word we used in those days. One night she stood outside in her nightgown. Stood out there throwing rocks at her house, breaking windows, before her husband could grab her, wrestle her back inside. After that she disappeared from the neighborhood. Two months, half a year, who knows? No one missed her. Things went on as usual. The father mowed the lawn. The son kept to himself. Husbands went to work. Wives vacuumed. All those years ago. But I can still hear the sound of the windows shattering. Sometimes I think I can almost make out what she was shouting.

Memories at the Movies

Malle's *Phantom India* makes you look at the vulture
feeding on the buffalo carcass, its featherless
fleshy neck smeared with blood, the entire screen
an image of curved hooking beak, ripping
and gulping bits of entrails. You look away,
cover your eyes, hoping the scene will change.
When you glance again, there's the bloated corpse
and flies and greedy inflamed eye of the buzzard
which now plunges its whole head and neck
into the buffalo's asshole, picking out coils of intestine.
The camera doesn't move, the film continues to scroll.
Eventually you have to look, you've *paid*
to see this mess, but the more you look the less
distant it is—the deeper into it, the more it becomes
un-ugly, becomes just bird feeding on body,
until you're cleaned out, gutted, empty inside yourself,
fighting back all those memories of her,
of being in this same theater, shoulder
to shoulder in the dark, deep into *Les Enfants
du Paradis, Jules et Jim*—all unreeled at last now,
the film coiling on the projection floor as you sit
in the present with your head plunged
into memories, the way love will leave you,
unspooled, the way you become your own vulture
tearing and feasting on the past.

How Green the Leaves in Sunlight Are

On the phone with my friend who is having
a hard time with his life, who sits in a chair for days
holding a knife in his lap, who isn't able to talk
about it. It might be *bipolar*, but there is no word
for where he is. He is calling from the crack
between worlds, where the barrio of East L.A.
smacks up against New Asia, where the voices
he hears all day speak in tongues, and his life,
his other life, is lived in another country, *and what
do you know of it*, he asks, *what language do* you *speak?*
And I am listening hard, trying to piece it together,
trying to find the mystery of it, listening as I stare
into the green leaves of the plant outside the window,
and I notice for the first time that it's dying—
I look closer and see insects, tiny *grotesques*, colonies
of them, who've drilled their mouths into the veins
of the plant, whose bodies are the color of the leaves—
and it's hopeless, I'm thinking, everywhere it's
the everyday wreckage, the coming apart from within,
wormseed, Death smirking in the glaze of sunlight,
stroking the blade, Death who would have us
slit our throats with diamonds, whispering—*Do it,
do it, there's nothing here worth holding to,
you've already heard the story, all of it, you know
how it ends*—and what shall I tell my friend
whose voice drills into my skull, what new story,
what poem shall I construct, what should I tell him

about love, about how to pass through, tell me,
what shall I say about the crossing over, *bipolar,*
about what's on the other side of the crack,
about that island of ice and snow where the shades
hold out their cups, thirsty for what we bring,
our elixir, our mixture of honey and milk and blood,
our memories of how green the leaves are in the sun.

Lost Roads

I. DUNLAP CROSSING ROAD

This is the road between two rivers, a road through summer. On it, a boy is riding his bike. He believes he has all of time. At Dunlap Crossing he stops before the railroad tracks. On the other side there's a semi, a large meat truck, parked on the shoulder, and behind it, a police car. Someone should tell the boy—*turn back, ride away.* But he gets off his bike, crosses the tracks. The back doors of the truck have been sprung open. The boy peers inside. It's dark in there, and cool, like a cave. There are sides of beef hanging from racks. And emerging from the back, two policemen shuffle into sunlight, their blue uniforms soaked in blood. They are holding between them a man, helping him, his feet dragging, head lolled back, throat slashed. What do the policemen say to the boy? He feels a trembling in the earth. The crossing arms come down, bells jangling, and suddenly a train flashes past. A few passengers gaze out, disinterested, streaking into the future. The boy returns to his bike. He doesn't know what he is feeling. Does anyone know where he is going? He is on a new road, a lost road, a road without a name.

The boy and his mother are in a car, driving through the night. She is wearing an elegant black dress with a jeweled necklace. Her perfume, *White Shoulders*, fills the car. Perhaps to the boy the smell is visible, textured, like memories. Like poems. Where is the father, and the boy's twin brother? The mother is saying something to her son, but he's half-listening, looking through the windshield into the night. He's searching for stars, the ones he knows, the ones he might form into shapes, into constellations, Polaris and Ursa Major, Rigel, Orion the Hunter. From above you can see their car on Santa Fe Springs Road, traveling through the orchards, through the dark. And higher, the whole L.A. Basin, a great bowl filled with jewels. The boy is watching two islands of lights pulsing in the sky—one small, one large. They are crossing the night, approaching each other. He will remember this all his life. When the islands collide, they burst into flames. A small plane veers off, streaking to earth. The cargo plane comes down like a city on fire, a burning wreckage, breaking apart. Then there are ground fires flaring and smoking in the orchards. Thereafter the boy will feel in himself a dream of the night breaking open, stars falling. He doesn't know yet his mother will die young, that her death will be a darkness breaking apart within him, burning, all the years on fire spilling across his life. Later that night, the mother puts her son to bed, tucking the blankets around him. Is she crying? Her hair spills over him, her perfume. As he drifts off, he can see her necklace dangling, like an island of jewels, like stars, ones he cannot form into a shape, an unknown constellation, dazzling, a wreckage without a name.

Alchemy: Final Music

Death was some thing the old poems
sang about. *Timor mortis…*
Ubi sunt qui ante nos fuerunt?…
Carpe diem… Donne's portrait
in his shroud he hung above his bed
those last days. *Full fathom five*
thy father lies. Coral and eyes.
Worldes bliss ne last no throwe.
It wit and wend away anon.
Poets measuring with words
the wordless process the body
proceeds with. With night.
With mourning. Love labors against it,
losing. The mind over the years
gradually accedes, succeeds, perhaps,
in having a past to build from,
to place against. A negative. The image
appearing gradually from chemicals
in the dark, in the red light.
Like those songs. All the old poems
growing clearer as we grow older.

6

PLAINSONG

First Song

That long-ago morning at Ruth's farm
when I hid in the wisteria
and watched hummingbirds. I thought
the ruby or gold that gleamed on their throats
was the honeyed blood of flowers.
They would stick their piercing beaks
into a crown of petals until their heads
disappeared. The blossoms blurred into wings,
and the breathing I heard
was the thin, moving stems of wisteria.
That night, my face pressed against the window,
I looked out into the dark
where the moon drowned in the willows
by the pond. My heart, bloodstone,
turned. That long night, the farm,
those jeweled birds, all these gone years.
The horses standing quiet and huge
in the moon-crossing blackness.

Grandfather

Now I see you
in a small California town
asleep under fig trees, the black fruit
swollen and ripe. Your shadow seems
to deepen on the morning grass as peppertrees
scatter their leaves like rain
or seeds.

I remember a summer morning
we sat on your porch, the warped boards
pocked with holes and nails. The fields
freshly cut. The pond rimmed with willows.
You tried to tell me why my brown bitch
had eaten her young.
It was a morning of bees.
I saw the light sing on their wings,
a mellow gold quaking into music.
You must have heard, too,
for when I turned, you had fallen into a dream,
your throat humming with veins.

Then I heard that other music. The cicadas.
The green frogs. My bones
drained like the sap of trees
as I dreamed myself into the heart of the pond.
I forgot everything I ever learned.
Except your voice. Down there.
Singing of home, death, a blossoming tree.

Naming

for Sam Scott

Summer in the Tehachapi Mountains.
A broken waterwheel, its scoop troughs
splintered and empty. *Owl's clover.*
Rabbitbrush. Grandfather near the pond
pointing out the names of things —
Cottonwood. Manzanita. Rose quartz.
His voice full of tenderness.
It was the first time I knew words
as praise, as a way of seeing —
how the names bring things closer.

Near the end of my grandfather's life,
a stroke took away his speech. He would sit
on the porch, mute, and watch the sun
wear down the day.

But I remember the summers
when we picked *filaree*, stuffing it in our pockets,
where it coiled like clock springs.
We'd stroll back to the cabin at dusk.
Once we stayed late, watching dragonflies
dip over the pond. It was dark
by the time we reached the porch.
We could hear the men talking inside
and smell the potatoes and onions frying
in the black skillet. He put his arm around

my shoulder, and we looked up into the deep
catch of night, as slowly he began to name
the far-off, alien stars.

Memory

for Tim

It is dusk
on the bridle path that wanders
through the Griffith Hills.
Two boys walk, arm
in arm, under the branches of oak,
madrone, and pine.
They are brothers going home
before the sun goes down.
Walk with them. See
how the smaller, younger one
stretches his stride to keep
beside the other. They
talk quietly,
having spent the day searching for snakes
in the hills behind the bales of hay
slit with arrows the grown-ups shoot
for sport or hope. Why
do they stop before a tree
swarming with bees?
In the gnarled roots they see
an emerald lizard with spines
down its back. Don't wake them.
It's no dream as they dream
a kingdom to allow such a beast.

Crowned and golden, they continue
home, a sound of bells,
in the huge, quiet night.

In the House of Silk

When I was a boy
I dreamed in a house of stained-glass wings.
Each morning was a summer of listening—
the soft-tongued birds outside my window.
The opening flowers. I would lie in bed
and watch a breeze rustle the curtains.
I promised myself never to touch the words in my throat,
so my brothers never knew who I was
when we climbed the hills behind our house.

Once I spent a whole day
crawling through rotted leaves and ferns.
I came upon a clearing
where the sun laced some white-lipped ivy
and gold pollen eddied like snow
into the center of a spider's web.
I knelt until I found her
nestled against a leaf, face sparkling with eyes,
each skinny leg cramped under her
like crooked children at suck.

I wanted her to come out of the dark.
So I stabbed my tongue
through that thin carpet of silk
and drained from the moist threads
the inner gleamings of a spider's heart.
She would not come out.

I think she knew the flesh that tore her home
had no wings or eyes.
Or perhaps she felt the sudden cries of bees
swelling in my throat.

That night, my brothers asleep,
I rubbed my sticky fingers under the pillow,
and dreamed of women with silk hair,
and those small, needled mouths
that sewed my lips with kisses.

Portrait of the Artist as a Young Boy

The boy is making something
for the girl he has a crush on
he has taken an old panel of wood

and with a pencil draws an island
with trees a horse rearing up
flashing its hooves toward the sun

all of it surrounded by a sea
which he shapes in scallops and curves
then he takes a magnifying glass

and traces the pencil lines with
sunlight focused to a laser point
burning into the wood the outline

of horse and trees island and sea
he stops now and then to close
his eyes which burn as if

the drawing is being etched
through them seared
into his skull into his mind

which persists in its vision
forcing the boy back to his task
forcing the sun to char

the wood to brand the shapes
of the boy's world into the grain
that wants to catch fire

blaze up and burn into ash
what the boy would make of love
what love makes of him

First Kiss

was with Sonia in the closet
a summer morning her parents
off to work and the neighbor kids
were playing spin the bottle which
Sonia did and it stopped dead at me
so they pushed us into a closet
and there we were in the dark
muffled among the hanging clothes
nervous excited we didn't know
how to kiss so we just grazed
our lips and clutched each other
before opening the door to our
friends crowding around
as Sonia and I looked down
from our new height as if
we had glimpsed some secret
back there in the dark among
her mother's dresses her father's
stiff trousers something
unspeakable in the bodiless clothes
the empty sleeves and pant legs
dangling and brushing against us
ushering us closer together
in the perfume smell of
her mother the cigarette odor
and English Leather of her father
as Sonia and I grasped and swayed

our eyes shut tight as our mouths
in that first blind groping kiss
among the ghostly limbs clutching
and shuddering around us

Among the Immortals

Vernon shot Wesley in the back with a .22 rifle.
They were hunting rabbits in the scrub
along the Rio Hondo
walking single file when Vernon,
who was not always in this world,
just squeezed the trigger a little,
lodging a bullet in Wes's kidney.
Lucky it wasn't his spine! was what we said.
Lucky Wesley who got *SHOT!* and *LIVED!*
and at twelve years old became a legend.
In the showers after gym he let us see
his back where the bullet went in,
a blue scar the size of a fingertip.
We all stood together there,
water pouring over our bodies,
as Wesley told us how it didn't hurt, sort of,
he wasn't exactly afraid of dying,
I was afraid my DAD was going to kill me!
And Vernon, whatever happened to Vernon,
I'm thinking, writing this, Vernon
who had to find help, who had to run back
into the real world, just as I'm trying to find
my way back to the past, to a world
where no one ever died, where I stood
for a moment among the immortals
under the pouring waters of forever.

Coronach

The boat drifts along the shore.
My grandfather all his life
has waited for age to bring him
to this moment. He stops
to touch what he knows
of the earth growing for him
his last garden — the small bean plants
with their fresh, new leaves,
squash blossoms, pale shoots of corn.
The boat drifts with no one
aboard, dragging its anchor forth
and back through emptiness,
while all the sorrows
look out from shore
waiting for departure to begin.
My grandfather sings to himself
digging into the ground, preparing
his bed, as he dreams of flowers
that bloom in the dark,
of the boat with its small cargo of light
drifting
under the earth.

Robert McNamara (1876–1966)

2

I remember Robert
in a muddy field
outside La Conner
leaning against a fence,
stroking with one hand
the star-blazed forehead
of a mare,
in the other
holding out a windfall apple,
odor of sweet clover in the air,
Robert happy
in his Ish River country.
Isn't it clear,
he laughs,
these simple poems—
everywhere!
And pausing,
looks to the ground,
Besides—
how can we lose
with mud
on our shoes!

Robert Sund (1929–2001)

3

Your cotton blouse,
Debbie,
all its pearls undone,
your hair loose, the way
you opened your mouth,
the sounds you made, I can
still hear them, still see us
that time in our sweet
season, in our young
craving, your body
and my body, slow dancing
to the Moonglows,
eyes closed, dream dancing
over the abyss, Debbie,
you, whose hands held
the cup of trembling,
who drank the waters
of oblivion, all these
gone years, Debbie,
and you a shade
dancing among
the bodiless dead.

Deborah Perry (1944–1965)

4

This is the room
where John is dying.
This the Yorkshire sun
over the dales.
This the bramble of light
by Black Waterside.
These the syllables
singing the hours.
These the hours
dissolving in air.
This the fire
in the whiskey
on John's table.
In whose hands now?
In whose hands
the alms of days.
These are the Signs.
These the fields in flames.
Each spear of wheat a spear.
Every bush a burning bush.
In the room of the room
where John is dying.

John Sloan (1925–2000)

The Wonder of It
Ending in the World

for Ellen

The heart never fits the journey.
Always one ends first.

JACK GILBERT

I think ahead to that moment
silence has prepared for me
when I shall look back
and sing
how all that year we lay together
in the field through the nights
as the seasons colored us
as the trees blossomed
and the berries ripened into autumn
Our small, white house
with its windows and music
Your serene, gracious love
that opened my life
And I gave my heart
as my heart broke down
O my love

Poem to Han-shan

The place where I spend my days
is farther away than I can tell.
Men search for a way through the clouds,
but the cloud way is dark and without sign.

HAN-SHAN

Five years I've looked into this orchard
hoping to measure my life, only to find it empty
of me.
      If I could weave into my heart all the nights,
the gold oriole in shadows, the moon
inside each apple, the delicate jade-flower garden,
the song in the shape of fruit,
                or stone,
or rain. Dream.
      All dream. I weave nothing
these long days watching the leaves fall and the trees
holding on. And holding on.
          Outside my window
lilacs are opening, there are new blossoms
in the strawberry field, the splintery water-tower
is full and heavy in the sun. And now a hummingbird
streams from stem to stem of the fuchsia.
I don't move. Han-shan,
        finally I see
what has been given me.

As for Me,
I Delight in the Everyday Way

Han-shan

Each day the earth turns, each day
the sea rises, all the days the seasons
are, the small lemon in its own time,
a face turning from the window in an old house,
the song we can always
almost hear.
          There's a poetry to this life
no one will be able to write.
The horses come down the mountain at dusk.
We've all seen this. But who gives thanks?
And what about the lemon. When was the last time
any of us brought that sweetness
                     to our face?
Of each loss, there is an opening.
To find a voice for love is a way
of loving.
How all the griefs rush out of you
when you hold the little lemon in the cup
of your hand. How easy it is to forget
these poor daily rags we wear
shine as bright as the silks of kings.

Spring in the Santa Cruz Mountains
with Li Po

Here our life
is the absolute clearness after rain.
We sit in the middle of a path
near an acacia tree.
Under a rush of branches
where the stream pools,
a towhee dips its feathers,
shuddering water into jewels of light.
A squirrel shrills in the scrub oak,
furious we have come near
her throne of leaves.
We hear the long drone of a wasp,
far off,
near the sun.
Bees brush the yellow powder
of acacia blossoms.
Li Po says, "Imagine the taste
of that sweet honey wine."
This place is so many-tongued.
Blackberry vines wander through sage.
A strand of web
spins sunlight into silk.
It's no use to think here.
We are not important.
An ant tugs at my sandal,

the wind rises,
and we must go.
It's all beginning, Li Po,
dusk, mountains, the drifting clouds.
Once we part from here
who knows where
the river of years
will take us.

In a Lydian Mode

after Cavafy

NORTH BEACH, 1963

We met in Vesuvio's
among the night tribe drifting
from Toscas and City Lights.
I cannot remember her name,
or her room, only our suddenly
open bodies, the yielding,
the crossing over. I cannot
remember what we said after.
In that other time. Waking
to foghorns, mists, streetlights
opalescent through the windows,
those nights like crushed pearls.

HAIGHT-ASHBURY, 1965

A Victorian bathroom, incense
and candles, Erik Satie, hashish,
a bathtub, where I soak, steam rising,
and across from me, leaning back,
Diana, her hair wet, her nipples,
all of time drifting, one silver note
on a piano, and then another,
the *trois gymnopédies* which will
never end, which will go on
across time, sounding here,
in this place, now, in this body,
this memory making music of me.

Crossing the Island

Kárpathos, 1975

Heat heat and the sky a flame of sapphire
an ocean of fire even rocks blazing
the earth a rush of coals Aegean summer
the air still the day dead center in the sun
the world without breath even the goats
drinking light all morning have descended
to the shade of a cistern while out there
the blue of the ocean and the other blue of sky
come together in that place where the gods
descend to this world and enter
the heavy honey of the body and it was on
this day when I set out into the core of light
wondering what it would bring for I knew
for once and for good my marriage was over
and henceforth there would be only these excursions
into the sun into the body and the world
would exact its praise of basil or goats or the smell
of thyme and the resin and gold pitch of pine
and all the shelters of the spirit began crumbling
within me as I dismantled the man I was
learning to replace the old belief of Latin
with the new tongue of this world the tongue
of rock and mountain and memory of the woman
washing her hair on the terrace in the granite light
as I went through the day to the other

end of the island where the wedding guests
had butchered a goat and roasted the meat
over a fire in a noon so bright I couldn't see
the flames as if sunlight were searing the flesh
and the bride looked upon it all and found it
to her liking as the groom carved the meat
passed it around and we ate of this world
and so it would continue

Auvergne

Oc, Dieu d'amor
Quora me donas jòi, quora m'en ven dolor
RAMBAUD DE VAQUEIRÀS

Why should the mindless singing
of the mockingbird high in the avocado tree
so much please me? Or the lure of light
these winter mornings the first days of War? —
as our Century comes down.

I sit on a bench
reading the eight-hundred-year-old poems of a Sufi dervish.
So where is the Beloved Friend? Is it this dog
sleeping at my feet under the shadow of a cow skull
nailed to the fence?

I believe
I no longer believe in the romance of the body.
Once, twenty years ago, in that other country,
in Auvergne, I knelt down inside the fire.
Of my beloved, I remember most her quiet words,
the taste of comice, warm rain in the orchard,
our little happiness inside us. That's not the All
of it. Rumi says, *The price of a kiss from the Beloved
is your life. What a bargain!* But I was a thief,
I did not pay.

Like everybody,
like you, I returned from that country of love
alive. From nights of the Auvergne. The river Lot

with its shade trees in summer, arbors of dusty grapes,
white honey from the blossoms of rosemary,
fields where the dragon sang inside the writhing
mouths of poppies where the black seeds catch fire.

                                        Returned
to the mockingbird, crazed, singing out of season.
To my dog, stretching now, who turns
and shoves her snout over my book, jowls
slobbering on Rumi's ecstatic poem to the Beloved.

                                        What
does she know, this trusting, dumb creature
who forgives me everything? Is *the cure for pain*
in the pain? Grinning, tongue out, tail thrashing,
she knows something is up.

                                In the next Millennium,
among the nightmares and machines, among time's
indifferent slaughter of our body, there must be poems
to make room of silence, to praise birdsong in winter light,
to sing of Auvergne, the Friend, and the old promises of love.

Backyard Suite

I. A WINTER'S TALE

Eight crows
in the bare winter cottonwood.
Eight phantoms cawing at the merlin
regal and aloof on a high branch,
the crows furious he won't budge.
Eight corbies with sleek beaks
crowding around the king,
eager to pluck the agate of an eye,
black cloaks over hunched shoulders,
a jackdaw rage at the royal indifference.
Then the merlin turns his head
and with one imperial gaze
glares at the crow nearest him
who halts in midscreech, hops backward,
and sprawls into his gibbering clan
who turn their cries on their brother
and soon are nothing but crows again
cursing among themselves
as the merlin goes back
to the spoil of empire clutched in his talon,
into which he hooks his beak,
ripping out feathers, strips of flesh,
unstringing all the gems.

Rose, sister of Rue, toward the end wandered about the yard with little interest in the world, spending most of her time under the bird feeder where the siskins in their frenzy scattered seeds, showering over Rose food from the heavens, but she never looked up, having had enough of enough, and one night couldn't fly to her roost, so huddled in the straw, where the rat found her, and where we found her the next day, bloody and dazed, and Ellen took her in, fed her by hand, tried to keep her alive, and she did live, she came back among us, looking even more strange, feathers missing, eyes open in a shock of wonder. That was the fall I painted the house; climbing the ladder to the high windows and roof crown, I would look down on her, sitting under the feeder, seeds raining over her, just there, in her own time, where nothing would disturb her, not even the shadow of the hawk scattering the others, Rose oblivious of the fall sun through the cottonwood, the leaves on fire coming down, showering the yard, coming down over all of us, all of us under our own spell, wading through time, through the season and the fading sun, where Rose, sister of Rue, without complaint, closed her eyes, let go, showing us how it is done.

3. THE PERFORMANCE

A cold winter night, three raccoons
in the persimmon tree, three clowns
lurching around, branches sagging,
springing, the whole tree quivering—
at its top, the crown jewel, the last
and best of all persimmons, toward which
one raccoon makes his careful slow way
across a branch, reaches with two hands,
grabs, tugs hard, juggles it, teetering—
the other raccoons watch as this
knucklehead in his confusion lets go
of everything—persimmon, branch,
dignity—flips head over tail,
plunges through branches, snags
a limb, and hangs by his hands—
meanwhile the persimmon hits the ground,
and it's a race to see who can get it—
the smallest scoops it like a football
and begins on three legs to run—
which doesn't work—another
grabs it, loses it to the third, and they all
tumble down the road, the persimmon
bobbling among them like a moon
on fire, as into the night, scrabbling
and careening, they disappear.

Today I am sanding and painting window trim.
I will listen to no music.
I will pay attention.
With fingertips I touch the surface of wood.
I dust away the dust.
With a brush I apply primer.
Simple, careful strokes.
It says somewhere to make a joyful noise.
It says somewhere else, to find peace you must first
empty your heart.
Someone said when you meet Buddha on the Path,
murder him.
T'ao Ch'ien says, if offered wine, never say no.
Everyone is giving everyone else advice.
All these centuries, and what has changed?
They say Death is a dragon's claw out of the earth.
I say, I'm tired of all this talk.
Yes, I know, it's a dragon world.
Dazzling. Harrowing.
Nevertheless, today I am painting window trim,
mindful of each stroke,
working in my sometimes happy,
sometimes sad,
little life.

5. HAWK AND HEN

The day unseams itself, crows exploding the air, jays shrieking from the loquat, hens cowering under the deck, but no sound from the hen pinned to the ground in the talon of the hawk standing over her, who turns his head toward me as I approach, raising his wings to increase his size, does not want to let go, looks into me with pure fury, beak open, clacking his bony tongue, and when I step closer, the hawk lifts off, just rises from the earth, leaving the hen, a few wingbeats and he's on the ridge of the roof, bobbing his head, clacking again, the crows diving around him, jays screeching, but it's all winding down now, as I stoop and gather the hen, fluff back her feathers, on her back three deep punctures, blood beginning to seep, but she seems okay, so I set her down, and she staggers over to her sisters, as the hawk lifts off the roof and soon is above the levee, trailing a mob of crows, the jays now screaming at me as I walk across the yard and back into the day, into time, into whatever comes next.

6. ODE TO AN EARWIG

Well, bub, I hate to say this,
but you look butt-ugly,
you look like a Bosch nightmare.
No wonder you spend your life
under boards or hide in the rotten hearts
of cabbage on the compost heap.
Would Saint Teresa call you holy
with your oily little body
and those evil-looking tongs
at the tip of your tail
arching over your back as if you would
behead your own head,
earwig.
Even your name is ugly.
Is it true your true desire
is to burrow into the ear of a sleeper?
You little monster, no one loves you,
except Ellen's hens,
who come running from all over the yard
when I overturn a board,
and you and your cousins,
your lovers and brothers,
dash in mad directions,
scuttling everywhere
under the murderous beaks of the hens
who think you
a delicious morsel,

earwig, and up
you are gobbled.
Thence
in the immortal,
immense Way of the universe,
you are alchemized
in a hen's egg—
perhaps the very one
I've cracked on the edge
of a skillet
and am this morning
scrambling in an omelet.

7. HUNOLT STREET TABLEAU

This morning,
thumbing through Thucydides,
I stop and look out the window.
Two towhees splash in the birdbath,
water *frizzing* off them.
Below the bath the cat sits,
gazing up with green eyes.
A pair of doves huddle on the rooftop.
And hovering over the arbor,
a hummingbird, a shimmering ember.
For a moment everything's suspended—
embers, emerald eyes, jeweled beads of water.
Thucydides stops talking about the wars of the Peloponnese.
And my life hovers as well,
caught like words in the poem
of this momentary spell.

8. ODE TO BITTERNESS

Holding an egg with
one hand I crack
the shell against the lip
of a skillet, the yolk
drools into sizzling
butter as I stand
and look out
the window to the
feeder where three
pine siskins flick
seeds on the ground
which Ellen's hens
peck with a rapacious
greed and I flip the egg
over easy, bring a cup
to my mouth and taste
the bitter coffee I
hated when a boy and
my father let me sip
from his cup as he
sat back with a cigarette
squinting at me through
the smoke and through
the years now as the
seeds scatter outside
like rain that begins
to fall through this

morning in November
as I listen to the radio,
the president telling us
again why we are beginning
a war because no one
can quite believe him
and I can hear
my father's laugh
as I put the cup down
and say *bitter* and
he says *but you better*
get used to it—
the rain drizzles
outside as I turn
the radio off, furious
at the same old
new lies, scoop
the egg from the skillet
and begin to eat
with my father
dead all these years now
though it seems
he was just here
drinking the bitter
coffee he loved so much
he'd fill a thermos
and sip all through
the morning reading
the paper, raging,
his bitterness

eating him alive
over the lies
and rapacious greed
of this forsaken
world of horror
and strife—
Jesus H. Christ!
this—*you better*
get used to it—
bitter,
bitter life.

9. OH YES

Oh no—
now we're in for it, everything's slamming shut,
closing shop, the leaves on the cottonwood are crying
fuck it and letting go in the wind, the cold
is coming, winter storms are massing at sea,
morning ice on the deck and the dog skids off
in a blur of legs, then it rains and rains and rains,
and the plague is upon us, strange fevers and aches,
the body spelling it out, impossible to ignore,
you're in a machine consuming itself,
and this morning walking out, you look up
at the persimmon tree for the first time in weeks
and notice all the leaves are gone, and there they are—
persimmons—fiery globes, hosannas and lauds,
and you can't help yourself, admit it, even sick
and miserable, mired in the dreck of winter,
you reach out your hand, take hold of the fruit,
oh yes, there's another world, there's a sun
within the sun, yes, kindness is real,
oh yes, blessings are everywhere.

Simple Gifts

for Kirby, Anita, Mort, Dick & Sue, Nick & Sue

Let the young rain of tears come.
Let the calm hands of grief come.
It's not all as evil as you think.

ROLF JACOBSEN

Sometimes there are the hard days, the long nights,
wandering inside myself,
desolate, confused,
when I think of Kirby's old walnut tree,
its roots tangled in the leach lines,
how it struggles year
through year to bring forth its small crop,
and how we shuck off the fleshy green skin,
place the nuts on a rack to dry
for those winter nights when we'll sit
around the fire with friends, and talk
as we pour wine, slice the apples and cheese,
crack open the shells to eat the earthsweet
gnarled seeds.

Book of Psalms

for Mel Tuohey, Linda Kitz,
& Fred Levy

PLAINSONG

It got so
quiet
in the cabin
no voices
no music
even birdsong
gone
from the mountain
and with the snows
the silence
deepened
this was where
I lived
was how I came
to hear
what singing
is

Every afternoon that autumn
walking across campus
past the conservatory
I heard the soprano
practicing
her voice rising
making its way up the scale
straining to claim each note
weeks of work
of days
growing shorter
darker
storms slamming the campus
the semester staggering
to an end
everyone exhausted
drained
heading out and going home
the campus nearly deserted
but the soprano
still working the scales
when I passed under the trees
the liquidambars on fire
the clouds like great cities
sailing out to sea
and didn't I ascend
with her

my own weariness
and sorrows
dropping away
didn't we rise together
her voice straining
wavering
at the top of its range
almost reaching
almost claiming
that high
free-of-the-body
final note

LITTLE SONG FOR THE TEN THOUSAND
BODHISATTVAS ON THE KITCHEN TABLE

What's going on
with this string of sugar ants
flowing across the table
these miniature
beings
these little flecks
of incarnation
what's the universe
to them
that they inspect it
so carefully
grasping a tiny piece

in their jaws
bearing away each
sugary jewel
of melon
while above them
another being
watches
and what does he know
grasping
his own jeweled
moment
his own little
happiness
making a sound
that sounds like

singing

TO THE LEAST AS TO THE MOST BOW DOWN

All I can manage
this morning
is this little
cluck
of a song
for which
nevertheless
I am
thankful

BROWN TOWHEE

Everyone notices the stoop
of the hawk
the whirling jewel
of the hummingbird
we all love
the mockingbird
filling the yard with music
the low glide of pelicans
cresting waves
tanagers passing through
in the plumes
of tropical flowers
we marvel at the owl
exclaim
over the eagle
even the great ugly condor
riding thermals
above Big Sur
amazes us
with its enormous
grace
but you
little one
common one
brown towhee
no one
notices you

you're just there
in the background
somewhere
undistinguished
unknown
the unseen bird
bird I'm seeing now
looking through
my window
to the winter drizzle
the slums
of the sodden
desolate garden
the only bird
I can see
the only creature
out there
in the dregs of weather
my sweet
little secret
the drab
nondescript
one
and only
brown towhee

THE SUMMER THE SUMMER BURNED DOWN

Years ago
with Sherry
one honey
summer morning
through the orchard
to the charred rooms
the burned-out
farmhouse
where Sherry
showed me
pulling her dress
over her head
and letting it
fall
among the glitter
of broken glass
wasps
buzzing through
the window
crows outside
crackling their
song of black
cinders
the odor of
tarweed
and apricots
peaches too ripe

on the ground
all those summers
ago
Sherry
and the black
ash
of crows
Sherry and apricots
bursting their skins
wasps
charred singing
honey
honey

MEADOWLARKS AND HAWKS

A farm road
in the San Joaquin
heading into the red dirt
of the gold country
miles and miles
of fencerows
with meadowlarks
singing on the wires
the song of one
entering the song
of another

all down the road
window open
I hear song
trailing
into song
the road continuing
as far as I can see
and every mile or so
on top
of a telephone pole
sits
a red-tailed hawk
shoulders hunched
turning his slow
iron gaze
over all he claims
of the singing world

THIS OX, THIS BODY

Once more
to plow
through the gold
field of morning
under the weight
of sun
and when the day

is done
to drink from the trough
cold water
brimming
with stars

7

I WANTED TO PAINT PARADISE

GIOTTO DI BONDONE

(ca. 1266–1337)

In the piazza today at noon everything in a swirl of light. No shad-
ows. No hint of the spirit. All things in their shining forth. Too real.
Like angels in the Rose Window with the sun blazing through them.
Gianna's grapes on the table as if they had just been created. The
poplars on fire. The Arno like quicksilver.

When the bells ring from San Marco, I stop my work. I bow within me. Three times a day, I stop what I am doing, I let the bells fill my body. In the morning the bells are like silver, at noon like gold, in the evening the bells are emeralds. They ring, and they ring. They tell me how to praise — over and over they ring out how to be worthy of the work before me.

This morning on the Via del Cocomero, I was admiring a basket of oranges, when a pig broke loose from a passing drove, knocked over the basket, tried to dash between my legs, and knocked *me* over.

> Maestro, are you all right? the vendor asked.
> Yes, yes, I laughed.
> He was surprised by my humor.
> Pigs are very smart, I explained. All these years I've been
>> making thousands of lire with their bristles. I've repaid
>> them nothing, not even a bowl of swill. So, how can I
>> begrudge a little revenge?

And besides, how could I tell him, it was good to be down on the ground a moment. It's true I have painted basilicas in Rome. That some call me a Master. But brother Francis would love this story. To be brought to earth by a pig. To be down among all the other miracles, the oranges scattered about me like small suns, to be astonished once again.

To paint the body accurately is not enough, it must be made to occupy a credible space, not stacked like wood or floating above the world in some mystical suspension. The body must have depth, a dimension that cuts into the space around it. Like sculpture. There must be light and shadows. There must be a logic to the arrangement of figures in their landscape. The old man this morning scything wheat, the oak casting a pool of shadow, and behind them the hills receding farther and farther, diminishing to a point that vanishes. Can this be measured? Music has rules of harmony. Mathematics has its golden numbers. And for painting as well? Are there laws of dimension, of proportion and space? If there are chords of sound, might there be as well harmonies of light?

The dog whimpers in her sleep. She is chasing hares again—her paws scrabble against the floor, her tail twitches. Soon she will wake, and look around. She will come back to this world. I love looking into her eyes. They are amber, like a glass of moscato held up to the sun. I want that color for the dusk in the garden at Gethsemane. Topaz. For my painting of our Lord abandoned and weeping among the flowers.

Beppo thinks brother Francis was a fool. *To touch lepers!* But look at Beppo, my little crooked master of the broom, who sweeps the workshop, grumbles at the dog, angry there is no one who will touch *him.*

Maso asks me, of all paintings, which do I admire most. I remember years ago when I made the journey to Siena, with travelers from San Gimignano, some as far as Volterra and Arezzo. We had come to see the *Maestà* of Duccio di Buoninsegna. A painted altarpiece, tremendous in size. At its center, the Madonna, unlike any seen before. The architecture of her throne! How Duccio sits her on it, as if in real space. The Bishop proclaimed a holiday, the marketplace was closed, alms were distributed to the poor. Then the procession—with horns and drums the people bore the altarpiece to the Cathedral. One by one we approached, with candles, as the bells sounded. Maso, if you had been there! Such joy, the people wept. As if the Mother had come down among us, was *here*, that you might reach out, touch her.

The crow on Gianna's roof waits for just that moment when the child has turned away, then it drops down and has the crust in its beak and is off over the piazza toward the Baptistery. I think I hear laughter in its *caw*. Or perhaps mockery. The crow in my painting sits on the roof. Watching. It can make no sound. It cannot spread its wings like a miracle. It will never fly.

Taddeo wants to start right away on a massive panel. He wants to paint the Crucifixion. He has a vision of the Resurrection. I want him to learn how to make a brush. To use the soft hairs from Gianna's white hog, not the stiff black hairs from wild boars. I want him to crush burnt almond shells to make a rich black. To grind chicken bones into powder for a primer. (He can find some under the table.) I want to tell him—Before you can paint a panel, you've got to make one. Use the easy wood—poplars, linden, willows. I want to take him into the forest. I know where there's a seep in the hillside. If he scrapes it, he will find seams of many colors—ocher, rose, sinopia. If he wants to paint crowns, he must learn how to hammer gold into a leaf. For his sky, he will have to crush lapis lazuli. If he wants to paint Paradise, he must first find a pig.

The Pope wants me to come to Avignon. Visconti wants me in Milan. Every week a new summons, a new commission — paint this, paint that — flattery, money, huge blank walls only Giotto can manage, they say, come, Maestro di Firenze! Taddeo is miserable with ambition. He would paint them all. And more. Fame is a sickness in him. Nothing can fill him up. Even my sweet Maso is tempted by it all. Maso who is just now mastering the touch of joy on the human face. Who one day will learn the touch of grief. I am tired. Everywhere great cathedrals are rising. All this overreaching. This arch higher than the last. In Beauvais they say the choir will disappear in the clouds. What will hold it up? I remember the valley of Mugello, the stable in the Colle di Romagnano when I was a boy. The mud walls flecked with straw. Dirt floor. Roof beam sagging. I remember those nights in summer I would sleep out there. The dawn through cracks in the ceiling. The little hen huddled over her eggs in the corner, the secret nest my mother hadn't found. Our burro looking down on me as I woke on my straw bed. Looking down with her calm, sad eyes. No paintings. No banquets. No ambition. No pride. A world as simple as the Lord's childhood. Yes, brother Francis, I hear you. I was just a peasant boy. I knew nothing. I didn't even know how happy I was.

Gianna knows everything in the neighborhood. She knows every-
one's secret life. Even more than the priest. Father Arnolfo is a kind
old man. Too kind, too innocent. Something like you, brother Francis.
At Confession, the people do not wish to disappoint him. But
Gianna. She knows *all* our sins. Even before we commit them! And
her memory is long. Does she forgive us? Who can tell. But like many
others, I have longed for absolution with my head on her lap.

The great Byzantine Madonna—who can open his heart to her? So aloft, remote, so above everything. In Avignon it's worse—the court painters have turned her into a fantastic queen, bejeweled, draped in gaudy silks. My madonna would be the woman who walked among us. Would be as my mother, the one I could turn to, the one who tamed my father's wrath, who believed in goodness and kindness, who tried to make happiness in the world around her.

Dante stopped today on his way to Ravenna, on his way into exile. How bitter he has become, how angry his politics. But we get along. *How's the great poem going?* I ask him. *Who have you damned today?* He smiles, tells me he hasn't made up his mind where he will place *me* in the *Commedia*. In turn, I show him the frescoes I have begun in the Arena Chapel. I describe to him the Judgment wall I will paint—the saved on the right, the lost in flames on the left. We talk awhile, two old men, musing. *Send me the* Commedia *when you are finished*, I say as he's leaving, *and I will decide which side to place you on my wall.*

Every day I see the three blind men begging in the piazza near the Duomo. To be blind. My greatest fear. As you say, brother Francis, we should confront our fears. So, I practice it from time to time. I close my eyes. I touch the table. I pick up objects. I let my hands explain. I break open the pomegranate. I imagine jewels. I touch the walls of my fresco. How poor, how blind my paintings are. Eyes closed, I see how they might shine. I see a world lit from within. I see my poverty.

This afternoon, returning from a walk, I stopped on a hillside and looked down on the Arno. It was dusk, the river filling with the melt of sun, shimmering, like the long swirling tail of a dragon. I suddenly became dizzy. My body felt far away. I saw a star fall from the sky. There appeared a woman clothed with the sun, the moon under her feet, upon her head a crown of stars. I saw a dragon rise out of the river. There was war in the heavens. Michael and his angels fought the dragon, and it was cast out. It fell upon the Earth, as starlight, as sunlight, as hail and fire mingled with blood. And the Earth opened. I saw the Duomo come apart, crumble into the pit. I heard a voice crying *woe* to the inhabiters of Earth. I beheld a pale horse, and he who sat on him was Death. The sun became black and the moon became as blood. Every mountain was moved out of its place. The Kings of the Earth hid themselves in caves and said unto the mountains, Fall on us, hide us from the face of Him that sits on the throne, for the great day of His wrath has come. And I beheld a great multitude, who stood before the throne, before the Lamb. They were clothed in garments of the sun, crying with a loud voice—Blessing and glory and wisdom and thanksgiving be unto our God. That is what I saw. It lasted an instant. It lasted a lifetime. Then I was back, looking down on the Ponte Vecchio, the little boats on the Arno, the Duomo in the distance. I turned and walked back down into the city of men.

I see Maso's fresco, and I don't know where to look. His figures are expressive, but he does not place them well. I try to tell him—Maso, the work must instruct us *how* to see. There must be a purpose, give us a story, place the figures so there is drama, a tension. The details are fine, but make your people not so static. Let them touch each other, it's all right, rest the head of the child against the mother's breast. The incarnation is real, Maso, we live in a world of the flesh. Make it so in your painting.

Beppo laughs at the goat—*Look at that fool, he's eating flowers!* I don't remind him of his own favorite meal—Tuscan sausage—minced offal and blood pudding stuffed in the bowels of a boar.

The sun on the Arno, calm water, a reflection of the Ponte Vecchio, mirror of the two worlds. And now a boat, a man rowing upriver, the oars scooping sunlight, breaking the water into gold. People come from everywhere to see the work of Cimabue. Duccio. They come even to see Giotto. How amazed they are at the frescoes. What miracles, they say, what magnificence. And every night the true night showers them with diamonds. And every morning the sun spills gold into the Arno.

Maso asks me about the burros, why they appear so often in my paintings. I tell him of my childhood in Mugello, my few years of schooling, how difficult reading was, how impossible to make numbers make sense, my great shame as the slow one, the dense one, the one who drew pictures on walls. I tell him of our burro, my boyhood companion, the one who listened to my sad stories with his sad eyes. Yes, I have painted him often. You will see him bearing our Lord as He enters Jerusalem. And he is also there before the crib at the Nativity, the first of all creatures for the Infant to see.

I wonder, brother Francis, what you would think of the Assisi Basilica the Order has built in your honor. Did you not say to your brethren—*Beware, take care not to receive churches and habitations.* What would you think of the great frescoes of your life that are painted there? When brother Giles visited, he was enraged by what the Franciscans had permitted. The only man alive who knew you, he stormed at the brothers—"All you lack are wives. After throwing Poverty overboard, it is easy enough to throw Chastity as well." Ah, you preached a severe poverty, Francis. Perhaps too extreme. A blank wall may have served for you. But we are like children. We love the paintings, we need to have before us what our minds cannot see.

Beppo brought to the workshop today a human skull. God knows where he got it. I didn't ask. It sits there on the table, with its mocking smile, as if it knows some great secret. How elegant, how eloquent the architecture of bone, lucid, like a sculpture of the Mysteries, pale as moonlight. And in the caves of the eyes, a glimmering, the flickering ghost light of a presence.

How ambitious Taddeo is, and how impatient. I remember how it was. I remember working for Cimabue, my master. Let me do this scene, I would say, let me paint Joseph's face, let me put rubies in the angel's wing, let me... let me... Cimabue would frown—*Today you work on feet, just the feet of the crowd. And be sure to count all the toes!* One morning he left the workshop. I don't know what got in me. He had been working on a panel—Joachim among the shepherds. I went up to it, and I painted a fly on the cheek of one of the shepherds—delicate, perfectly detailed, a marvelous fly. That afternoon when Cimabue returned, I watched as he went back to work, saw him stop, try to brush away the fly, once, twice, before he realized my prank, my audacity, my skill. I was young, what did I know. He might have been enraged, he was the great Cimabue, this was a panel he had been working on for weeks. He looked over at me. *Come here, Giotto.* And I approached, waiting now for his wrath. But he laughed. *Very good,* he roared, he clapped my shoulder. *Nicely done, Giotto. A good lesson for me. And now a lesson for you—erase it, make the fly disappear, make it so no one can ever tell it was there.*

From the hills above Florence you can look down and see fields, orchards, the Arno, the Cathedral, streets, houses. From above how simple and ordered it appears, as if part of a great plan. From up here there is no Gianna, no Maso, no oranges in the marketplace, no lamentation from the churchyard. From this distance the piazza is without life, no sounds of argument, no laughter, no bells. From up here, away from it all, amid the light and the sky and the quiet, a world we can look down from, but where we cannot live.

Taddeo insists the Florentine painters are better than the Sienese. It is not an issue that interests me. When I look at Guido and Duccio, the masters of Siena, I see *più bella che si può* — as beautiful as possible — an exquisite beauty, sensual, charming. Among the Florentines there is perhaps less exaggeration, something more vigorous, serious. The Sienese serve beauty. The Florentines seek truth. One is not better than the other. There are many paths.

No one is allowed inside the courtyard of Giovanni di Fiesole. Often I have walked before it, have wondered what it is like inside. Everyone knows of his wealth. We have heard rumors of his collection, mosaics from Byzantium, bronze jars from the Orient, pottery painted with fantastic animals, silk brocades of paradisal colors, a stone lion older than the Pantheon. Giovanni hoards it all. It is just as well. We pass by his house with our minds on fire, imagining wonders, while he sits in there, alone, surrounded with ashes.

Today in the piazza, Beppo drove his oxcart into a rut, the cart tipped, and he was tossed into the mud. To everyone's delight. Even Beppo laughed. I look at all my work. No clowns. No laughter. All those worlds I have left out.

Someday Taddeo will be a Master. And Maso. From them will come others. And so it will pass on. Will there ever come a one who finally gets it right? Can there be a painting like a Tuscan night? A fresco of a summer in the Mugello. Will there ever be a work that will open in us a morning like those mornings in Umbria, the poppies heavy with dew, lark song, the sun rising as if the first day of the world?

Benedict XI wanted to make St. Peter's the most glorious church in all Christendom. He sent agents throughout Umbria, Tuscany, Ravenna—to seek out the finest craftsmen, the best artists. One came to Florence, came to my workshop, asked for a sample of my talents to bring back to the Pope. I laid out a parchment, dipped a brush in red paint, and drew a perfect circle. Take this to His Holiness, I said. The agent was outraged. This is a mockery, he sneered, am I to have no other design but this? When Benedict received it, I am told, he clapped his hands. He smiled. Bring me Giotto, he said. And thus with a single stroke I entered Rome.

One day the Can Grande della Scala summoned me to Verona. To his magnificent court—musicians, poets, scholars, artists. Dante had passed through, had recommended me. And so I came. And so I witnessed a man with power, who commanded the lives of people, whose wealth was astonishing, a man of large sympathies, much learning, who loved the arts. But also a man of cruelty, greed, a man who ravaged other cities, ruthless, a man who wished to build an empire. And what did he want of Giotto? He wished me to paint. Not a massive fresco, not a biblical scene. He desired that I paint—*him*—life-size, exact in every detail, a kind of painting never done before. And so I began. I had him sit for me. An hour every day when his time permitted. I worked in silence, and listened to him talk. Politics. Strategies. Intrigues. I remember his anger at the feud of two important families, the Montecchi and the Cappellati, a rivalry that threatened to spill over into public carnage, disrupt his rule of the city. He would speak to me of these matters as I made his portrait, as I brought him to life on a wood panel, something for his vanity, that his visage would be known through time, for all to stand before and marvel, his power so great that even Death must bow before him, must kneel down.

Gianna knows nothing of art, but she is my finest critic.

Giotto, does no one ever smile in your paintings? Is the
world always so sad? Put in some children. Doesn't it
say—*Where there are children, you will find the Kingdom*? I
know there is a time for weeping. But isn't there as well
a time for gathering, a time for singing?

Both Taddeo and Maso want to begin a New Jerusalem. They want to paint the structure of the vaults of heaven, great columns of light. Monolithic. But I no longer want what will dwarf the human. *All* these works, in time, will crumble, will come down. Those who would know my signature, let them find it in the fragments. In the way I paint the poppy. Or the ear of this burro. A leaf. A face in the crowd. Let them seek me in the small, the common. Let it be the everyday psalms where they find me.

I must confess a secret. I have placed myself in one of my paintings. No one will ever notice. It's one of the panels in the Arena Chapel, the one showing the Lord, surrounded by disciples, entering Jerusalem on a burro. In the background, away from the crowd, there is an olive tree, and in it a boy is climbing out on a branch. He is high in the tree, leaning out. He will not fall. He is just a peasant boy. All he wants is to see.

This morning, two ravens in the piazza. Two shadows. The fountain. Fresh cream with strawberries. I can hear the plainsong of monks in the chapel of San Marco. Today I am going to paint the face of our Lord down from the cross. Today I must paint the dead Christ. Yes, brother Francis, I will put you among the disciples around the body, among those grieving—the one looking down whose face is streaming tears. For the weeping Veronica, I will use Angelina whose son was crushed by an ox. For Joseph, I will use Pascual the cabinet-maker as he stood over the grave of his wife and newborn. I will make him an old man. For a flower, I turn to the flower. For the faces of sorrow, I need only look within, open the Book of Grief, where all of us have our stories.

Taddeo keeps asking me about Paradise. What do I know, I tell him. But he persists. He wants me, he wants *us*, to paint it. I've tried. In the Arena Chapel, above the Last Judgment, two angels unscroll the blue dome of heaven, and beyond it you can glimpse the towering walls of Paradise, hammered from gold, encrusted with gems. But it's just craft. I have no vision of it. Taddeo thinks I am a great painter. That my works exalt both this world and the next. I must tell him—they are nothing. They are like holding up a candle in daylight—a tiny candle held out under the enormous Tuscan sun.

I will not work today. I'm tired of painting Great Scenes. I'm going to go into the wine cellar. Then Beppo and Maso and I are going to sit under the arbor and watch the Arno, watch swallows skim under the Ponte Vecchio. We're going to drink wine, eat *funghi trifolati*, Beppo's specialty—porcini in olive oil, with garlic and parsley. Beppo will tell us of the wives and priests, about the harvest, how the young men don't work hard anymore. We'll talk, and there will be nothing about marvels or angels, just the common tales of our ordinary days, this simple life.

Taddeo has been telling me about the fruit trees in his new painting, how perfect they are, how their fruit will last for hundreds of years, better than the originals, he says, that fall to earth, that perish. Sometimes, Taddeo, I believe you're an idiot. You'd rather paint a plum than eat one.

On the Vespignano road, many years ago, two old men with switches trailing a white ox lumbering through sunlight and through shadows on a Tuscan summer day. Who appear here now, on this wall I am painting, in this church beside the graveyard where they are buried, and where the white ox lumbers on through the country of light.

Yes, brother Francis, I wanted to paint Paradise, a great city, a city structured like music. But look at this rosemary on my table. The bowl of grapes. A cup of water. The iridescent feather of the quill I am using. The stone wall outside my door, wild basil growing in the cracks. The smell of geraniums. The lizard sunning itself on a stone, bobbing up and down with happiness. The blue door to Gianna's house across the yard. Her rooster with his bloodred comb. The bells of Santa Croce and the bells of San Marco and the bells of Santa Maria Novella. The sparrows Maso scatters when he walks from the stable. A puddle brimming with light. The lake above Fiesole, full of sun all day, filled with starfall at night.

8

WHEN THE STARS BEGIN TO FALL

Provenance

I want to tell you the story of that winter
in Madrid where I lived in a room
with no windows, where I lived
with the death of my father, carrying it
everywhere through the streets,
as if it were an object, a book written
in a luminous language I could not read.
Every day I left my room and wandered
across the great plazas of that city,
boulevards crowded with people and cars.
There was nowhere I wanted to go.
Sometimes I would come to myself
inside a cathedral under the vaulted
ceiling of the transept, I would find
myself sobbing, transfixed in the light
slanting through the rose window
scattering jewels across the cold
marble floor. At this distance now
the grief is not important, nor the sadness
I felt day after day wandering the maze
of medieval streets, wandering the rooms
of the Prado, going from painting
to painting, looking into Velázquez,
into Bosch, Brueghel, looking for something
that would help, that would frame
my spirit, focus sorrow into some
kind of belief that wasn't fantasy

or false, for I was tired of deception,
the lies of words, even the Gypsy violin,
its lament with the *puñal* inside
seemed indulgent, posturing.
I don't mean to say these didn't
move me, I was an easy mark,
anything could well up in me—
rainshine on the cobblestone streets,
a bowl of tripe soup in a peasant café.
In my world at that time there was
no scale, nothing with which
to measure, I could no longer
discern value—the mongrel eating
scraps of garbage in the alley
was equal to *Guernica* in all its
massive outrage. When I looked
in the paintings mostly what I saw
were questions. In the paradise
panel of *The Garden of Earthly Delights*
why does Bosch show a lion
disemboweling a deer? Or that man
in hell crucified on the strings of a harp?
In his *Allegory of the Seven Deadly Sins:*
Gluttony, Lust, Sloth, Wrath, Envy, Avarice,
Pride—of which am *I* most guilty?
Why in Juan de Flanders' *Resurrection
of Lazarus* is the face of Christ so sad
in bringing the body back to life?
Every day I returned to my room,
to my cave where I could not look out

at the world, where I was forced into
the one place I did not want to be. In
the Cranach painting—behind Venus
with her fantastic hat, her cryptic look,
behind Cupid holding a honeycomb, whimpering
with bee stings—far off in the background,
that cliff rising above the sea, that small hut
on top—is that Cold Mountain, is that where
the poet made his way out of our world?
My father had little use for poems, less use
for the future. If he had anything
to show me by his life, it was to live
here. Even in a room without windows.
One day in the Prado, in the Hall
of the Muses, a group of men
in expensive suits, severe looking,
men of importance, with a purpose,
moved down the hallway toward me,
and I was swept aside, politely,
firmly. As they passed I glimpsed
in their midst a woman, in a simple
black dress with pearls, serene, speaking
to no one, and then she and the men
were gone. *Who was that?* I asked,
and a guard answered: *The Queen.*
The Queen. In my attempt to follow
to see which painting she would choose,
I got lost in one of the Goya rooms
and found myself before one of his
dark paintings, one from his last years

when the world held no more illusions,
where love was examined in a ruthless,
savage anger. In this painting
a woman stood next to Death, her beauty,
her elegance, her pearls and shining hair
meant nothing in His presence,
and He was looking out from the painting,
looking into me, and Death took my hand
and made me look, and I saw my own face
streaming with tears, and the day
took on the shape of a crouching beast,
and my father's voice called out in wonder
or warning, and every moment
I held on made it that much harder
to let go, and Death demanded
that I let go. Then the moment
disappeared, like a pale horse, like
a ghost horse disappearing deep inside
Goya's painting. I left the Prado.
I walked by the Palacio Real with its
2,000 rooms, one for every kind
of desire. I came upon the Rastro,
the great open-air bazaar, a flea market
for the planet, where everything in the world
that has been cast aside, rejected, lost,
might be found, where I found Cervantes,
an old, dusty copy of *Don Quixote*,
and where I discovered an old mirror,
and looking into it found my father's face
in my face looking back at me,

and behind us a Brueghel world
crowded with the clamor of the market,
people busy with their lives, hunting,
searching for what's missing. How casual
they seemed, in no hurry, as if they had all
of time, no frenzy, no worry,
as the Castilian sun made its slow
arch over us, the same sun
that lanced the fish on crushed ice
in the market stalls, fish with open mouths,
glazed stares, lapped against each other
like scales, by the dozens, the *madrileños*
gaping over them, reading them
like some sacred text, like some kind
of psalm or prophecy as they made
their choice, and had it wrapped in paper,
then disappeared into the crowd.
And that is all. I wanted to tell you
the story of that winter in Madrid
where I lived in a room with no windows
at the beginning of my life without my father.
When the fascist officials asked Picasso
about *Guernica:* "Are you responsible
for this painting?" he looked back
at them, and answered slowly: "No.
You are." What should I answer
when asked about this poem?
I wanted to tell you the story of that winter
in Madrid, where my father kept dying, again
and again, inside of me, and I kept

bringing him back, holding him for as long
as I could. I never knew how much
I loved him. I didn't know that grief
would give him back to me, over
and over, I didn't know that those
cobbled streets would someday
lead to here, to this quietude,
this blessing, to my father
within me.

Rooms

Remembrance belongs to them
that were here.

ALKMAN

The stars and the rivers and waves
call you back.

PINDAR

For the world must be loved this much
If you're to say "I lived."

HIKMET

What if you could live
in a cowslip's bell. Like Ariel.
Or like the bee who nudges its way inside
and emerges burnished with pollen.
Look—
a hummingbird plunges its head into a blossom
for a taste of nectar. The Lord said—
In my Father's mansion there are many rooms.
Take your pick. All the spirits
grieve for the room we call
body. They want to dwell
among us, they want to taste and see.
It's said Christ entered the room
named *Jesus.* And when that body
was crucified, he cried out—*Father,*
why have you forsaken me? What

if we could live in *this* world. I know
of a field in the San Joaquin with vernal pools,
lupine, owl's clover, poppies.
I know where there's a hive in the live oak
where you can taste wild honey.
Last night my brother told me he was so unhappy
he wanted to die. He would take his life
if he had the strength. Once, years ago,
my brother found a snake on a canyon trail,
a tiny ringneck snake the color
of the earth on one side, the color
of fire on the other. He held it
in his hands. Held it out like a gift.
Like wonder. A small thing, perhaps,
but maybe that memory helps keep him
here. I remember one morning
on the Manikarnika Ghat where the bodies
were burning. I watched
a man step up to a pyre and with a club
break open a skull, scattering
ingots along the banks of the Ganges,
releasing the spirit, it is said, so it might pass
from this collapsing room
to the next. *In my Father's mansion
there are many rooms.* One
I return to often—memory takes me
to a farmhouse surrounded by orchard
in the valley that is called the Pajaro.
I watch the morning light through the windows
as it finds the couple in bed,

two small people asleep in each other's arms—
I watch as he wakes and gazes at her
as I gaze now, at the two of them—
how young we were, how little
we knew of what would happen—
too soon the seasons turn,
to other arms, to other rooms.
The day's on fire! Roethke cried.
But it's raining outside, it's April, the rain's
pelting all the blossoms—still,
Roethke's right—if I look
I see a slow writhing flame nothing
can put out, a fire burning inside
the day, inside the rain, a flame like silk
the bees brush against
inside the flower, the hummingbird's throat
burnished with embers—
the day's on fire! the night's on fire!
all the rooms are burning!
Keats in his death room, feverish, saw a flame
pass from one candle to another,
like a spirit, and to Severn
cried out—*Lift me up—I am dying.*
If you walk in the Roman cemetery
you will find his stone
carved with the words—
Here lies One Whose Name was writ
in Water. He is buried
in a room deeper than time.
I think of Emily's room

as she stood in throe and transport,
in radiance, in the terror
and the cleaving, in the Hour of Lead.
Like Emily, my brother
is not among the members of the Resurrection
untouched by morning, untouched by noon.
My brother can barely live
in his body. In his room. What then
of the rooms in paradise?
When you look out the window
what do you see? I see
a cottonwood beginning to bud, I see
a skeleton higher than a house
that soon will quiver with leaves,
with the green fire of summer. I believe
it is easy to love summer's vast
sumptuous room. But how to love
what can't be imagined? Death's
quantum world, with its rooms
within rooms, with its doors
to nowhere, or elsewhere. How to imagine
my brother's room, a camper shell
on a pickup in the City of Angels
where he drives looking for a place
to park, to spend the night,
where no strangers, no policemen
will rap their knuckles against his shell,
roust him. *Who can be coming*
to the edge of my gates
at this black hour of night?

Last night the sound of an owl
in the cottonwood.
I took a flashlight, shined it
up through the limbs, and there he was—
a great horned owl, looking down
on me. When at last I turned
and walked away, I could feel
his eyes on my back.
You have made me forget
all my sorrows.—Of thee
I stand in awe. In Shay Creek I stood
looking down at an owl, its eyes
being eaten by ants, more ants
seething from its beak, so many
syllables
trying to get at it—
the rooms within, once luminous,
now empty, the light
going out across the stars, they say,
the deep journey back to provenance.
My brother says—*Yes*—he would like
to see once more the stars
of our childhood—deep summer,
when pollen drifted across the lake
turning to gold the blue water at dusk
and we saw for the first time
Orion rise and drift across the night,
his body in flames over the black water.
Journeys and odysseys. Rimbaud's
voyages. His return from Aden,

his *thirteen days of sorrows,* carried ashore
on a stretcher, his knee the size of a gourd—
Where are the treks across mountains,
the rivers and the seas, O Voyager,
O Outcast? On his last morning,
he woke to the brilliant sun
in his room, the sun he loved,
and he cried to his sister—
I am going under the earth, but you,
you will walk in the sun.
Pindar says—*Blessed is he*
who has seen these things
and goes under the ground. He knows
life's end. He knows the empire
given by the god. But what
of the empire managed by men?
What of Nazim Hikmet whose room
for thirteen years was a cell? Who
every night waded in water and pulled nets
out of the sea, the silver fish mixed
with the stars. Who every morning
imagined his execution—*The poplars*
are blooming in Ghazali, but the master
doesn't see the cherries coming. That's why
he worships death. Close your hand—
the daylight inside your palm
is like an apricot. One day the guards
came for him, came to his room,
and brought him outside
for the first time. He was amazed

by how far away the sky was.
While Nazim was in prison, he wrote
Things I Didn't Know I Loved.
He names them—*sun, trees, roads*—
the list is long—*sea, clouds, rain, night.*
What is it, I wonder, I didn't know
I loved? I didn't know how much I loved
my brother in that canyon years ago.
I didn't know how much I loved
the earth and the rivers and the stars,
all those mornings opening
into bright rooms. I didn't know how
love would cross the years
to here—to this place I have prepared
for my brother—this poem,
this room where he may live.

Letter to Robinson Jeffers, Big Sur Coast, Winter 2005

I will go down to the lovely Sur Rivers
And dip my arms in them up to the shoulders

I will touch things and things and no more thoughts

ROBINSON JEFFERS

Robin,

It's a storm-driven day of light and clouds
and wind and sea and scurling waves.
Tor House still stands, and Hawk Tower,
and the surf still slams the headlands
as when you first came to this wild coast,
as it did ten thousand years ago.
Our century of perpetual war and genocide
has ended at last — now the Nightmare
of the future as relentless as the surge
of the sea is gathering around us.
As you predicted, governments rearm,
the age of tyrants returns, and America
has thickened to Empire. It is *our* sword
raised over the smaller nations of the world.

This morning at Tor House I looked out
the window of your death room
to the sea as ever there as it was for you,
all things in the great ebb and flow,

in the tide pulse of waves
that make shape of time. I confess
I sought your ghost in the rooms
you made of stone, conjured your shade
in the narrow hall and winding stair
of Hawk Tower. From there Una
would watch you stalk the shore in storms
and return drenched, return to the pull
of words you sought to make a dwelling of,
as lasting, as carefully placed as the granite
of Tor House and Hawk Tower.

We must uncenter our minds from ourselves.
How else to see the unhuman beauty of things.
Some say we will not outlive this new century.
A cunning, rapacious cancer, we will consume ourselves.
And bring down everything. Nothing will be spared.
We are attending the death of a world, it is said.
No longer will hawks hover in thermals over Big Sur,
the great whales with their songs will disappear,
and over all this wild coast, over Point Lobos,
over Tor House and Pico Blanco, the waters
of the world will rise, and your Tower, Robin,
will be nothing but a heap of stones crumbling
in the green ghost rooms of a vacant, dead sea.

It's winter here.
The wind blows spumes from wave crests.
Heraclitus said all is process, all
is fire, is rock, sky, and sea, each life

its own singularity—sea spit, sea foam,
the emerald fires of waves breaking on rocks.
To stand on these headlands is to witness
great forces, what you called an inhuman beauty.
I have walked these coastal mountains
looking for the glade where the deer lay down
their bones, that secret place of refuge you found.
Once up Sobranes Creek I came across
the skeleton of a deer in the limbs of an oak,
dragged there by a cougar years before,
the bones polished clean by storms and sea winds,
white ribs like columns of a temple, the tower
beyond tragedy thrown down by the savage god
of the world.

Below these cliffs
cormorants hunt like wolves,
the silver fish flash like knives
in the green undersea light,
hawks wheel over the plunging cliffs,
a kestrel cries *kree kree kree*
and all the songbirds hush.
I think of the storm-struck music
your bones were molded to be the harp for,
a Lear on the outcrops of Big Sur, mad
in the mad wind, harping of what is
and what will be the end.
In this place as an old man you once
lay down to rest, and saw through
half-shut eyes a vulture circling over you,

and you imagined how it might be
to be the feast of a buzzard, that ugly bird,
eater of the dead—what honorable work,
you said, and lucky the man to have his bones
picked clean, to be alchemized in that wild blood,
and rise into the sky toward the sun.

They call you unbeliever, Robin.
True enough, you had no faith in humanity,
no trust in abstractions or the shams of dogma.
Your hatred was hard and clear and cold.
Rock and hawk were your totems.
But you did believe in a god,
a wild god who *is* this world, this universe.
Only one light is left us, you said, the beauty
of things, not men, the immense beauty
of this world, a transhuman intrinsic glory.
Here the sun goes out over the sea,
and night builds its kingdom, more vast
than seasons, builds its black terraces,
its high throne of stars. Our atoms
were forged in the engines of stars,
in the core of suns. So then, Robin,
we *are* creatures of light, and in the end
are driven like stars into the night.

By the Rivers of Babylon

for my brother Tim & my twin brother Mike

I walk the levee of the San Lorenzo,
a midsummer afternoon,
walking to the clinic for the lab results.
I see the heron wrapped in its shroud of silence,
shoulders hunched, standing over a pool,
gazing into its still spirit.
This day my blood will be translated
into an alphabet spelling *no going back.*
This day with the ashes of my mother in the Pacific.
This day with the ashes of my father in the Sierra.
What are you waiting for? *What are you waiting for?*
Never before the arc of the hummingbird
like a streaking evanescent jewel.
Never before this world so translated from plural to singular.
Not the leaves of the cottonwood,
but each leaf,
dazzling with light.
I walk to the clinic
where the doctor waits with his map of the future:
the body, the body,
the elemental process of the body—
to be trolled for, to take the lure,
gladly,
baited with worm,
the line dangling from the great cloud ship of myth,

to be caught
and held squirming and gasping in the tight body,
then released, tossed back
into the glittering, streaming river
of this day.

ॐ

I crossed the Mekong at dusk,
the outskirts of Vientiane —
in the street a car on its back,
an immense scarab, its carapace in flames,
black oily smoke smudging the sky,
and everywhere soldiers of the Pathet Lao.
In the morning
I woke with sunlight shattering through cracks in the walls,
splinters of light,
the room sheathed in cobwebs,
like a cocoon of silken fire.
In the marketplace
the Royalists and Pathet Lao laid down their weapons.
I looked into a bucket pulsing with toads,
another squirming with what appeared to be intestines —
eels with tiny eyes and needled teeth.
On a table the hacked pieces of a large lizard.
Everything of this earth as food,
what we put into our mouths,
the flesh of crabs,
mangoes, cow tongue, words...

We strolled the banks of the Ganges near the summer palace.
We could see smoke skirling downriver
from pyres on the Manikarnika Ghat.
Günnar talked of his pilgrimage to Bodh Gayā,
of his studies in the secret tantras of eros.
He had meditated under the bo tree.
He had seen a body rise.
We all wanted miracles.
The Ganges, sluggish and muddy, offered nothing.
We wandered the chowk,
lost in its labyrinth of alleys,
loud processions bearing corpses to the river,
sadhus smeared with ashes chanting *Rama nama satya hai*—
the name of God is truth,
or so Günnar translated it.
Just as we tried translating the scrawl of human smoke
unscrolling above the burning ghats—
Death opens the flower.
The body's marriage burns down.
The flowering bride wakes in the long corridor of ash.
And so

I hold my father in the elemental form of ash
where the granite river of the Sierra plunges into the Mojave.
Black bear, cougar, coyote in these mountains for thousands of years

where my two brothers and I have come together.
Below the Paiute graveyard overlooking the river canyon
Tim scatters our father's ashes to the South,
the North,
to the bluff where the sun rises,
to the West.
A sudden wind
and the ashes gust back over us,
dusting our faces and clothes,
a faint smell and taste of my father in my own body,
in this blaze of flesh,
these three flames of men burning out of their lives,
fathering in each other the elemental love
of brother for brother.

౨

I walk the levee of the San Lorenzo
where the river empties into the sea.
Thinking of my father.
Thinking of my mother whose ashes years ago were strewn
over these waters.
She lives only in the minds of a few now,
and soon there will be no one alive
who knew her,
she will no longer walk in anyone's dream
as I walk now along this shore
while miles out and deep underwater
on the edge of the Monterey trench
something monolithic moves in darkness,

silent,
plunging huge and fast.
And above it the killers,
orcas,
arc the surface,
a pod hunting together
down from Canada
tracing the song and spoor of whale.
I walk the levee under the long arc of the sun
with all my past streaming through me,
those mornings of light, the cottonwoods
with their ten thousand tongues murmuring of summer
and the slow burning of seasons.
I walk along the river,
towing it all
huge and singing
into the alchemy of this day.

Notes and Acknowledgments

Matar la Noche (page 12)

    matar la noche: "To kill the night," a phrase citizens of Madrid use to describe the nightlife of their city, which lasts until dawn.

Hacedor (page 13)

    hacedor: The maker, the artist.

In the Maze Garden of the Generalife (page 16)

    Generalife is the summer palace of the sultans above the Alhambra in Granada.

Altair and Vega Crossing the River of Heaven (page 20)

    Altair and Vega are the brightest stars in the constellations Aquila and Lyra, which come into conjunction for one night each year. They are known as Weaver Girl and Shepherd Boy in Japan, and are the subject of many love poems. The *Man'yōshū* is the earliest collection of Japanese poetry, containing 4,516 poems, compiled in the late eighth century. Kakinomoto no Hitomaro, one of Japan's greatest poets, lived in the seventh century.

Die Schwermut (page 24)

    die Schwermut: "Despair," the title of a poem by Georg Trakl (1887–1914).

The Words of Chilam Balam (page 24)

    Chilam Balam: "Jaguar Priest/Prophet"—Mayan prophet of Apocalypse who lived to witness his prophecy with the coming of the Spaniards. *The Books of Chilam Balam* are all that have survived of the principal sacred texts of the Mayans.

Lazarus in Varanasi (page 25)

    Varanasi (formerly Benares) is India's ancient, holy city on the west bank of the Ganges in Uttar Pradesh. The burning ghats (steps) are the location of the funeral pyres where Hindu devotees are cremated and their ashes strewn in the Ganges.

Closing This Year's Anthology, I Think of Radulfus Glaber... (page 27)

    Radulfus Glaber was an eleventh-century Burgundian monk and chronicler who traveled between monasteries observing and recording events of his time.

Memory: Quonset Hut, Rodger Young Village, 1947 (page 29)

Rodger Young Village was a Los Angeles public housing project for WWII veterans and their families. No trace of it remains today—where there were once 750 Quonset huts, you will now find the Los Angeles Zoo and the convergence of the Golden State and Ventura freeways.

Earth Angel (page 31)

"Earth Angel" is the title of a song by the Penguins, a rhythm and blues group of the fifties.

Melancholy Lu Yu Returns from the Graveyard (page 32)

Lu Yu (1125–1210) is the most famous of the Southern Sung poets. A prolific writer, he destroyed nearly all of his poems written before middle age; still, we have the more than ten thousand others he managed to write.

Praxis (page 34)

Kokinshū (or *Kokinwakashū*) is the first imperial anthology of Japanese poetry, compiled in the tenth century by Ki no Tsurayuki and others.

Waking on the Shining Path (page 36)

Ayacucho is a Peruvian city in the Andes within the territory of the Marxist guerrilla group Shining Path.

Love like a Catch of Fire (page 38)

Lady Izumi Shikibu and Prince Atsumichi were part of the Imperial Heian court at the turn of the tenth century in Japan. Their great love was celebrated in many poems to each other.

These Nights, Passing Through (page 38)

Netania Davrath is a soprano who recorded *Songs of the Auvergne*, orchestrated by Joseph Canteloube (Vanguard Classics OVC 8001/2).

Our Blood Is Red Coral... (page 41)

The title is a sentence from Nikos Kazantzakis (1883–1957). Kárpathos is a Greek island in the Dodecanese.

Signatures (page 53–64)

This group of poems is dedicated to the memory of Stan Rice (1942–2002), classmate, soul brother, "red to the rind"; a master poet of the generation born in the 1940s.

The Room Above the White Rose: Vientiane is the capital of Laos. Pathet Lao: Communist forces that overcame the Royalist army in 1975.

Paradise: Vajrasattva is the Buddha of Diamond Light, whose music is ice and snow, wind and water, and whose mantra is "renounce all attachments."

Dancing with Machado (page 68)

Antonio Machado, along with Juan Ramón Jiménez and Miguel de Unamuno, is considered one of the founders of modern poetry in Spain. When Leonor, his young wife, died, Machado moved to Baeza, where he taught school and lived a solitary life for many years.

The Birdcages of Oaxaca (page 71)

extranjero: Stranger.

Into the Dragon (page 74)

Though I traveled through much of Southeast Asia in the 1970s and 1980s, it wasn't until 2001 that I made my first trip into Vietnam, twenty-six years after the war. DMZ: Demilitarized zone, a 10-km-wide zone running east–west along the Ben Hai River, dividing the northern Democratic Republic of Vietnam from the southern Republic of Vietnam. It was the most savage battle zone in the war. UXO: Unexploded ordnance; it's been estimated that up to 30 percent of the ordnance dropped in Vietnam failed to detonate. Since the end of the war, 9,000 civilians, mostly farmers and children, have been killed or maimed when coming into contact with UXO.

Country of Clouds (page 85)

Fan Si Pan is the highest mountain in Vietnam.

Home. Autumn. The Signatures. (page 90)

Jalalabad is a city in Afghanistan situated below the Khyber Pass; the moment referred to in the poem occurred in 1975, before the Russian invasion, the Taliban takeover, and America's "war on terror."

Homage to Life (page 99)

A translation of Jules Supervielle's "Hommage à la vie."

Ode to the Smell of Firewood (page 101)

A translation of Pablo Neruda's "Oda al olor de la leña," from his *Odas elementales.*

Autumn (page 104)

Ōtomo no Yakamochi (718–785) helped compile the *Man'yōshū*. For a superb discussion of his life and work see *A Warbler's Song in the Dusk*, by Paula Doe (University of California Press).

Burning the Leaves (page 105)

I can think of no greater introduction and background to the art of haiku than R.H. Blyth's four-volume *Haiku* from the Hokuseido Press.

Of Sappho / [fragments] / Sabi (page 109)

Sabi (Japanese) is the patina, the character, the stark beauty that time gradually works into an object.

Steps to the River (page 111)

These versions are derived and adapted from the translations of Professor H.H. Ingalls (*Sanskrit Poetry*, Harvard University Press) and Professor George L. Hart (*The Poems of Ancient Tamil*, University of California Press).

Alam al-Mithral (page 124)

alam al-mithral: Arabic word with no equivalent in English; refers to the "place" where images exist.

Homage to George Mackay Brown (page 131)

A cento, in parts, for George Mackay Brown (1921–1996), the marvelous poet from the Orkney Islands.

Homage: Doo-wop (page 137)

The Moonglows was a rhythm and blues/doo-wop group of the 1950s. See also the note for "Earth Angel," page 346.

In the Stream Pavilion (page 152)

Yang Wan-li (1124–1206), Chinese poet from the Sung dynasty and a garrulous companion in the high country, particularly in the Jonathan Chaves translation: *Heaven My Blanket, Earth My Pillow* (Weatherhill).

On What Planet (page 154)

The title is from Kenneth Rexroth.

Drinking Wine with T'ao Ch'ien, Looking into the Fire (page 167)

T'ao Ch'ien (365–427), also known as T'ao Yüan-ming, was a farmer-recluse

whose unadorned, candid style was a major influence on the great T'ang
dynasty poets. He is known as "the grandfather" of Chinese poetry.

To Han-shan (page 182)

There are no certain dates for Han-shan other than late eighth century to early
ninth century, and there is even some conjecture that the poems attributed to
him were actually written by several persons over a few centuries. Neverthe-
less we have the poems, which depict a recluse-poet living at Cold Mountain,
from which he took his name. Burton Watson, one of Han-shan's finest trans-
lators, offers this summary of his poems: "Underlying them throughout is the
Zen—or more correctly, the Mahayana Buddhist—conviction that these very
experiences of daily life painful or peaceful, harsh or serene, are the stuff that
enlightenment is made of. There is, in other words, no Way outside of the way
of everyday life" (*The Columbia Book of Chinese Poetry: From Early Times to the
Thirteenth Century*).

Death in the Tehachapis (page 187)

Tehachapi is the region where the Sierra Nevada descends to the Mojave.

The Death of Lorca (page 213)

See *Federico García Lorca: A Life*, by Ian Gibson (Pantheon), and *García Lorca*, by
Edwin Honig (New Directions).

In a Lydian Mode (page 251)

"Trois Gymnopédies" are three piano pieces composed by Erik Satie
(1866–1925).

Auvergne (page 255)

Auvergne is a region in France that was once part of Occitania, where twelfth-
century Provençal troubadours composed the first lyric poetry in a modern
European language. Rambaud de Vaqueiràs was an early troubadour.

I Wanted to Paint Paradise (page 281)

Giotto di Bondone, commonly known as Giotto, was the master Italian
painter of the fourteenth century. Though the iconography of his frescoes is
Christian, the spirit that infuses his work is a deep sympathy for the human
condition, which he depicted with a realism, candor, and depth of feeling
that had not been realized by the painters before him. In Giotto we find the

beginnings of a humanism that would become one of the distinguishing marks of the Renaissance.

Francis of Assisi (brother Francis), canonized in 1228, was the subject of many of Giotto's paintings.

Maso di Banco and Taddeo Gaddi were disciples of Giotto who went on to become significant painters in Florence.

Duccio di Buoninsegna was the greatest painter from Siena, a master of the older Gothic style, and a contemporary of Giotto.

Arena Chapel, also called the Scrovegni Chapel, is the site of Giotto's great masterpiece, a fresco cycle of forty paintings. After seven hundred years (and nearby aerial bombings in WWII) it still stands in the city of Padua and may be visited today. One of the world's sacred places.

Cenni di Pepo, better known as Cimabue ("oxhead") because of his stubborn pride, was considered the greatest painter of Florence prior to Giotto. According to legend, Cimabue came upon the young Giotto herding sheep and sketching pictures on rocks, recognized his talent, and took him as an apprentice.

The portrait Giotto made of Can Grande della Scala has not survived. What has survived is the story of the two quarreling families, the Montecchi and the Cappellati, whom Shakespeare immortalized three hundred years later in *Romeo and Juliet*.

Provenance (page 323)

puñal: Dagger.

Palacio Real: Royal Palace.

madrileños: Citizens of Madrid.

Rooms (page 329)

Manikarnika Ghat is the main location of the funeral pyres in Varanasi.

"Who can be coming to the edge of my gates at this black hour of night?"—Apollodoros.

"You have made me forget all my sorrows"—Alkaios.

"Of thee I stand in awe"—Alkman.

"Thirteen days of sorrows…Where are the treks…"—Rimbaud.

"The poplars are blooming…"—Hikmet.

By the Rivers of Babylon (page 340)

Bodh Gayā is the place in Bengal where Siddhartha Gautama attained enlight-enment under the bo tree.

The chowk is a labyrinth of alleyways in the old section of Varanasi.

Index

About the Author

Joseph Stroud was born in 1943. His work earned a Pushcart Prize in 2000 and has been featured on Garrison Keillor's *Writer's Almanac*. In 2006 he was selected by the Poet Laureate of the United States for a Witter Bynner Fellowship in poetry from the Library of Congress. He divides his time between his home in Santa Cruz on the California coast and a cabin in the Sierra Nevada.